TODAY'S CHALLENGE TO TOMORROW'S VISION

A STUDY OF FACILITIES CONDITIONS AT SCHOOLS OF THEOLOGY

Walter A. Schaw

with
Ron Cason

Daniel Conway

Milton Ferguson

Christa Klein

Joseph O'Neill

Jerry Schmalenberger

Maureen Sepkoski

Floyd Simmons

Foreword by Fred Hofheinz

A JOINT PROJECT OF:

APPA:
The Association of Higher Education
Facilities Officers
&
Lilly Endowment, Inc.

Today's Challenge to Tomorrow's Vision:
A Study of Facilities Conditions at Schools of Theology

A joint report by APPA and Lilly Endowment, Inc.

Printed in the United States of America.
International Standard Book Number: 0-913359-65-3
Library of Congress Catalog Card Number: 91-77585

The opinions and findings expressed in this report are those of the authors and do not necessarily reflect the opinions of APPA or of Lilly Endowment, Inc.

Printed on acid-free paper

Contents

FRED HOFHEINZ

Foreword

In the context of the many demands clamoring for the attention of today's theological school leader, concerns about roofs and gutters, sidewalks and heating systems, may appear to be those most easily set aside for another time. Maintenance, after all, can be deferred precisely because it need not capture attention at this moment. This report, and the research upon which it is built, serves as a thoughtful correction to that presumption.

As the 1990s began, we at the Lilly Endowment heard increasingly from presidents and trustees at schools of theology that they were becoming preoccupied with the troubling issue of how to deal with the maintenance of aging physical plants. We knew about *The Decaying American Campus: A Ticking Time Bomb* (Rush, 1989), which estimated higher education's deferred maintenance backlog at $60 billion. We wondered how theological schools, not part of that study, might compare with other institutions of higher education.

After consulting with a number of leaders at schools of theology, as well as other trusted advisors, we decided it was time for the Lilly Endowment to develop a program to aid theological schools in this area. As a first step, we invited a representative group of forty-one North American schools of theology to help us explore the scope and magnitude of the problem. We provided grants to each school to support information gathering about their facilities conditions, and to assist in developing a process of comprehensive planning to begin to deal with these issues.

Then, we quite naturally turned to APPA to seek assistance in compiling and interpreting the data provided by these institutions. As Walt Schaw points out later in this report, this proved to be an exciting and rewarding partnership for APPA and the participating schools. The report builds upon the extensive data gathered from this cooperative effort, and provides information of invaluable importance for administrators, trustees, and all who care about the future of theological education.

It is important to view this series of grants within the larger context of the mission of the Religion Division of the Lilly Endowment, which is "to work with religious leaders and researchers to generate information, develop the insights, nurture the practices, and sustain the institutions needed to make available to the larger culture religious resources upon which a flourishing and humane society can depend." In service to that mission, the Endowment has long committed itself to sustained work with theological education institutions throughout North America.

We at the Lilly Endowment believe that the maintenance of the physical plant is not merely a matter of bricks and mortar, but must be seen in the context of a school's stewardship of physical resources. The quality of space, whether in a classroom, dormitory, or chapel, profoundly affects the quality of learning and campus life. Attention given to the decisions concerning facilities, then, is a deeply spiritual activity deserving the best efforts and fullest attention of all charged with the care of these precious resources.

One of our objectives in this work is, in the words of our mission statement, "to help secure the long-term viability of a strong and appropriately diverse constellation of theological schools." We profoundly hope that this APPA/Lilly study will serve that end.

Contributors

Ron Cason
Assistant Development Director, Church of God School of Theology, Cleveland, Tennessee

Daniel Conway
Director of Special Projects, Saint Meinrad Seminary, Saint Meinrad, Indiana

Milton Ferguson
President, Midwestern Baptist Theological Seminary, Kansas City, Missouri

Fred Hofheinz
Program Director, Religion, Lilly Endowment, Inc., Indianapolis, Indiana

Christa R. Klein
Program Consultant on Seminary Governance for Lilly Endowment, Inc., York, Pennsylvania

Joseph P. O'Neill
Principal Research Scientist, Lilly Ministry Project, Educational Testing Service, Princeton, New Jersey

Walter A. Schaw
Executive Vice President, APPA: The Association of Higher Education Facilities Officers, Alexandria, Virginia

Jerry L. Schmalenberger
Professor of Parish Ministry and President, Pacific Lutheran Theological Seminary, Berkeley, California

Maureen Sepkoski
Vice President, Administration and Finance, Catholic Theological Union, Chicago, Illinois

Floyd Simmons
Vice President for Business and Finance, Covenant Theological Seminary, St. Louis, Missouri

Acknowledgments

APPA: The Association of Higher Education Facilities Officers wishes to express its appreciation to Lilly Endowment, Inc., for its foresight in initiating and sponsoring this study. The Endowment's support, encouragement, and enthusiasm has been consistent since the project began in August 1990. We particularly thank Craig Dykstra, Vice President for Religion, and Fred Hofheinz, Program Director, Religion, of Lilly Endowment, Inc. for their personal involvement and support. Also at Lilly Endowment, we thank Peggy Fowley for the many hours she devoted to logistics for the site visits and workshops.

We also wish to thank the forty-one APPA member volunteers, listed in Appendix B, who served so ably in the on-site evaluations of facilities conditions and management at the selected schools of theology. Their written reports provided invaluable insights, not only for appraisal purposes but also in providing an understanding of the special circumstances at each campus.

We are truly grateful to the forty-one schools of theology who participated in the project since its inception, and who also are listed in Appendix B. While the data presented in this report is representative of all 202 theological institutions in the United States and Canada, the willingness of these forty-one to share rich detail and participate fully in the workshops has been critical to this study.

Special thanks is also given to the many institutions in addition to the original forty-one, who participated by responding to the final research instrument and provided a quantitative base of high statistical validity.

We also wish to recognize the Organizing Committee, several of whom served as workshop faculty, advisors, authors, and consultants throughout the project:

Larry D. Beloat
Christian Theological Seminary
Indianapolis, Indiana

Daniel Conway
Saint Meinrad School of
   Theology
Louisville, Kentucky

Norman E. Dewire
Methodist Theological School
   in Ohio
Delaware, Ohio

David P. Harkins
Eden Theological Seminary
St. Louis, Missouri

David L. Hodde
Archdiocese of Indianapolis
Indianapolis, Indiana

Fred Hofheinz
Lilly Endowment, Inc.
Indianapolis, Indiana

Charles W. Jenkins
Saint Mary's University
San Antonio, Texas

Wayne Leroy
APPA
Alexandria, Virginia

Joseph P. O'Neill
Educational Testing Service
Princeton, New Jersey

Walter A. Schaw
APPA
Alexandria, Virginia

Winthrop M. Wassenar
Williams College
Williamstown, Massachusetts

Special thanks to Dan Conway and Joe O'Neill, who served not only as faculty in the workshop series and as chapter authors in this report, but who also gave advice and counsel throughout the project. We are also indebted to the many seminary presidents whose encouragement and leadership have been an inspiration.

It is appropriate to recognize that this report represents an extension of the body of knowledge about facilities conditions, which has grown exponentially since the publication of *The Decaying American Campus: A Ticking Time Bomb* in 1989. Sean Rush, Partner, Coopers & Lybrand, has continued to give leadership in this field, as have pioneer scholars Harvey Kaiser and Hans Jenny, whose lone voices a decade ago warned us of the inevitable consequences of neglecting the facilities asset.

Among APPA staff, Wayne Leroy has been a partner throughout the project; Steve Glazner offered advice and support; Tina Myers kept operations on schedule; and Fran Pflieger's editorial and production management skills are reflected in this report. Thanks also to Jan Burt of the ERIC Clearinghouse on Higher Education for her help with the bibliography; the staff of Scott Photographics, Inc. for design, typesetting, and production; and Tim Dilli of United Book Press for printing.

These acknowledgments are but a brief summary of the efforts of many who not only responded superbly throughout this study, but also evidenced a belief that this work would contribute to the well-being of theological education. APPA came to this project hoping to make a contribution; we received more than we gave.

WALTER A. SCHAW

Introduction

This study provides an assessment of the condition of campus facilities at 202 schools of theology in the United States and Canada. It is the culmination of a joint project conducted by APPA: The Association of Higher Education Facilities Officers and sponsored by Lilly Endowment, Inc.

The original project included an initial assessment of facilities operations at forty-one theological schools in the United States and Canada, which began in June 1990. Presidents, business officers, and facilities managers were engaged in a series of workshops during the project. An important part of this first phase was an on-site evaluation of conditions and operations by APPA member experts, who then issued formal reports.

The scope of this first phase included issues related to solutions for facilities needs, including values of stewardship, decision-based planning, financial management, and trustee roles, as well as baseline information developed from reports and observations. With the success of this phase, the project was extended to encompass all theological education institutions, and this research commenced in June 1991.

The first three chapters reflect not only the research results, but a continuum of learning and evaluating, much of it resulting from a learning experience about facilities by all of higher education.

Chapter 1 reports a series of quantitative findings from the research conducted in the second phase of the study. Appendix A, Technical Notes, augments this chapter with specifics about how the findings were compiled. The presentation of data in Chapter 1 is intended to raise the appropriate issues for each institution. Throughout this report, terms such as "good" or "poor" are intended as objective measures, a value to apply for future planning, rather than judgments about past performance. Indeed, firsthand observations of the operations at theological schools reflect a high degree of dedication to doing a great deal with severely limited resources.

Chapter 2 is a collection of on-site qualitative observations at the forty-one campuses in the original study. The comments included were gathered from reports by APPA evaluators and, in some cases, from formal facilities conditions audits. This chapter does not quantify, but presents observations to give meaning to the data in Chapter 1.

Chapter 3 explores two concepts essential to ensuring facilities equilibrium at schools of theology, and to higher education institutions in general: 1) the need to accurately assess facilities conditions as a basis for sound planning, and 2) the value of using a financial planning model to ensure the continued health of facilities. The adoption of these concepts will not only help schools measure and correct existing facilities conditions, but will provide a framework for preventing the further accumulation of deferred maintenance.

In Chapter 4, Joe O'Neill presents financial perspectives for the renewal and replacement of facilities at schools of theology. The concepts of earning, borrowing, and giving are explored in the context of the typical theological school. Solutions, including denomination-wide campaigns for funds, are examined.

The challenge posed by deferred maintenance requires a new understanding of stewardship, and in Chapter 5, Dan Conway applies this ancient spiritual principle to the care of facilities. He calls for a new understanding of stewardship as it relates to each institution's human, financial, and physical resources.

Christa Klein reviews the critical role of trustees in Chapter 6, suggesting ways for them to offer leadership and expertise in support of the institution's mission.

Chapters 7 through 11 are case studies gathered from selected participating schools of theology. The authors of these chapters—two presidents, two business officers, and an assistant development director—each faced distinct challenges at their respective schools. They provide examples of success stories resulting from the APPA/Lilly project, as well some sound approaches to solving deferred maintenance problems.

This report has been developed for those whose support is essential for the future of schools of theology—presidents, trustees, and constituent groups. It is also intended to help those with financial and facilities responsibilities, including the business officers and facilities managers. *Today's Challenge to Tomorrow's Vision* presents vital elements in the successful preservation of each institution's largest capital asset, and an assurance of the facilities component for their mission.

WALTER A. SCHAW

CHAPTER 1

Facilities At Risk

"We must recognize our responsibility to coming generations who stand to lose the most if we continue to defer our problems rather than solve them." (Dillow, 1989)

Facilities at schools of theology in the United States and Canada represent a full range of conditions. While some are new and others are well cared for, many reflect a degree of deterioration that threatens the institution's ability to fulfill its mission.

Beyond the issues of teaching and learning, of health and safety, is the impact of facilities on attracting students and faculty, and, inevitably, on the financial soundness of the institution. A chronic lack of funds, fluctuating enrollments, and demographic shifts have all had an effect on facilities at many schools.

The primary purpose of this report is to identify the most significant questions an institution must ask about its facilities asset before it can develop effective strategies to reduce or eliminate the potential risk to those facilities.

Quantifying the Need

This section of the study has four objectives:

1. To recognize the value of facilities as an institution's largest capital asset.

2. To quantify, in dollars, the condition of that asset by measuring the magnitude of capital renewal/deferred maintenance (CRDM) needs at schools of theology.

3. To determine space utilization and its relationship to facilities conditions.

4. To examine the relationship of operating budgets to facilities conditions.

Facilities represent a $3.5 billion capital asset for theological education institutions. This value is derived by first determining how much space is represented by facilities. The chart below defines the distribution of space represented in the survey; the average space per campus has been calculated to be 187,149 square feet.

Universe of Theological Facilities in the United States and Canada

Number of Institutions: 202
Enrollment: 56,000
Full-time Equivalent (FTE): 38,150

Gross Annual Expenditures:

TOTAL:	$611,163,020
AVERAGE:	$3,025,556
PER FTE:	$16,020

Facilities Operating Expenditures:

TOTAL:	$84,340,494*
AVERAGE:	$417,527
COST PER FTE:	$2,211

*Includes utilities/excludes construction

How Much Facilities Space?

37,804,098 Square Feet

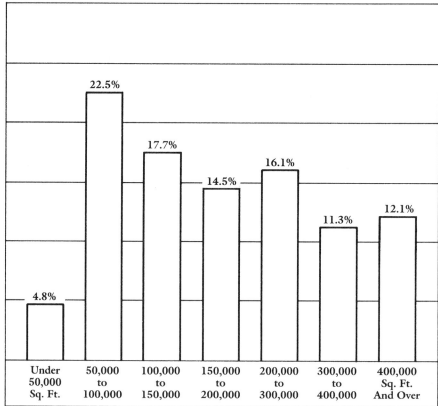

Mean Per Campus:
187,149

Median: 180,738

Sq. Ft. Per Student (FTE): 990

Based on U.S. averages in 1990, a conservative estimate of replacement value is $93 per square foot. Therefore, the total square feet of space for 202 institutions (37,804,098) multiplied by their replacement value produces an aggregate value of $3,515,781,000.

The CRDM backlog at schools of theology is $385 million. An average of $1,906,825 in CRDM needs per institution has been established by the study. Much of this data was derived from detailed audits of facilities conditions. The following chart presents the range of CRDM conditions reported.

How Much CRDM Backlog?

$385,173,600

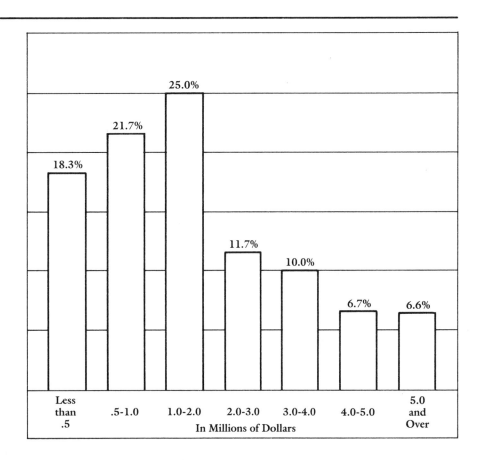

Mean: $1,906,825 Per Institution
Median: $1,464,450

CRDM and Replacement Value: The Key Relationship

The ratio of CRDM needs to total replacement value is the essential relationship in evaluating the severity of CRDM. This ratio can be given a numerical value by applying the standard APPA/NACUBO/SCUP Facilities Condition Index, or FCI (Dunn, 1989). Using this system, backlogs of outstanding work are ranked from "good" to "poor," as shown in the chart below.

It is worth noting here that while facilities pose a critical issue for many schools of theology, the average ratio of CRDM against replacement value of 11 percent is well below the 20 percent average for all of higher education reported in *The Decaying American Campus: A Ticking Time Bomb* in 1989.

Good, Fair, or Poor

Rating By Facilities Condition Index (FCI)

Mean: 11.0 (Fair To Poor)
Median: 10.4

Note: The conditions of about 36 percent of all institutions are "good" or "good to fair," but nearly 30 percent are "poor."

$$FCI = \frac{Cost\ of\ Deficiencies}{Current\ Replacement\ Value}$$

Example:
Institution Y has 200,000 square feet of facilities. Its value at $93 per square foot is $18,600,000. The CRDM Backlog is $1,860,000, or 10 percent. The Facilities Condition Index (FCI) is "fair."

Source: Sean C. Rush et al.,
Managing the Facilities Portfolio.

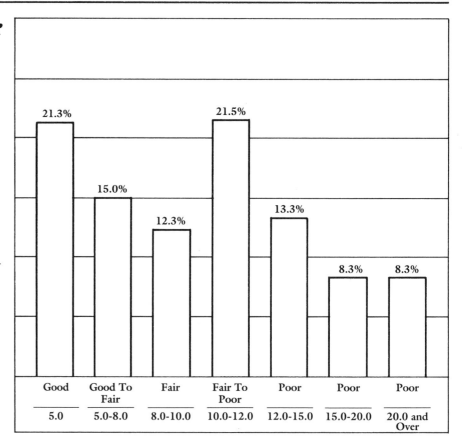

	Good	Good To Fair	Fair	Fair To Poor	Poor	Poor	Poor
	21.3%	15.0%	12.3%	21.5%	13.3%	8.3%	8.3%
	5.0	5.0-8.0	8.0-10.0	10.0-12.0	12.0-15.0	15.0-20.0	20.0 and Over

Housing represents the largest single category of CRDM needs at schools of theology, a reflection of changing student populations from single male to older, married, and/or female students. The following chart represents both aggregate and average CRDM reported by major category of facilities use.

What Kinds of Facilities Are Affected By CRDM?

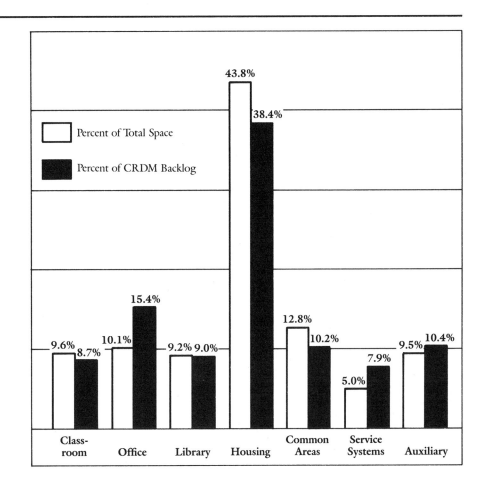

□ Percent of Total Space

■ Percent of CRDM Backlog

	Classroom	Office	Library	Housing	Common Areas	Service Systems	Auxiliary
Percent of Total Space	9.6%	10.1%	9.2%	43.8%	12.8%	5.0%	9.5%
Percent of CRDM Backlog	8.7%	15.4%	9.0%	38.4%	10.2%	7.9%	10.4%

Priority One: Service Systems

Institutions were asked to identify priority needs—those posing a risk of much higher costs and disruption of the academic cycle. Service systems, including boilers and heating and air conditioning systems, ranked first in the study, followed closely by concerns for primary structures, such as roofs of buildings, and safety. Much lower ranked were secondary structures such as windows, and functionality. The following chart summarizes the ranking reported.

Priorities for CRDM Needs

A ranking of first or second priority on a scale of one to five was given by institutions responding as:

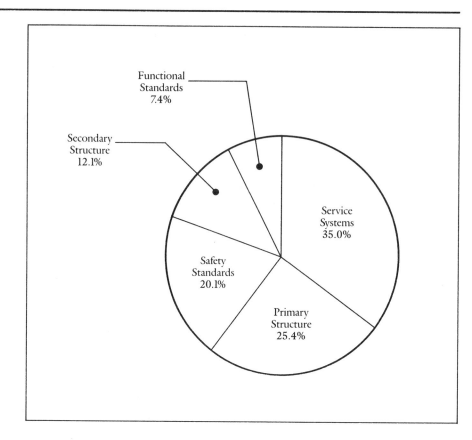

Functional
Standards
7.4%

Secondary
Structure
12.1%

Service
Systems
35.0%

Safety
Standards
20.1%

Primary
Structure
25.4%

Critical Variables

The data indicates that three factors have a significant influence on the extent of reported CRDM backlogs: building age, space utilization, and facilities operating budgets.

Building Age

Given that the average lifetime of a building is fifty years without major maintenance, some of the institutions that ranked in the FCI categories of "poor" or "poor to fair" also had some of the oldest buildings. The following chart reflects this relationship.

Does Average Age of Buildings Relate to Facilities Condition?

Average Age of Building Per School	Facilities Condition Index							
	5.0 or less	5.0 to 8.0	8.0 to 10.0	10.0 to 12.0	12.0 to 15.0	15.0 to 20.0	20.0 or more	Average
25 years or less	50%	16.6%	8.3%	8.3%	8.3%	8.3%	-0-	6.2
25 to 50 years	23.8%	9.5%	19.1%	4.8%	23.8%	19%	-0-	10.1
50 years or more	23.8%	-0-	5.9%	5.9%	17.6%	11.8%	29.4%	14.7

The data above clearly relates the average age of buildings to facilities conditions; while the data illustrates age as an indicator, not an absolute, it is noteworthy that *all* of the institutions with the most critical CDRM backlogs by FCI also have buildings averaging 50 years or more in age.

Space Utilization

There is a wide variance among respondents in the ratio of space to enrollment. Some differences are accounted for by factors such as whether the campus is residential, has a large library serving as a denominational resource, or serves a population composed of many married students. Some institutions have low space-to-student ratios because of serious declines in their enrollment over the past twenty years. Comparative data on space, full-time equivalent (FTE) enrollment, and average CRDM by category is shown in the next chart.

How Much Space Per FTE Student?

Expressed in Square Feet

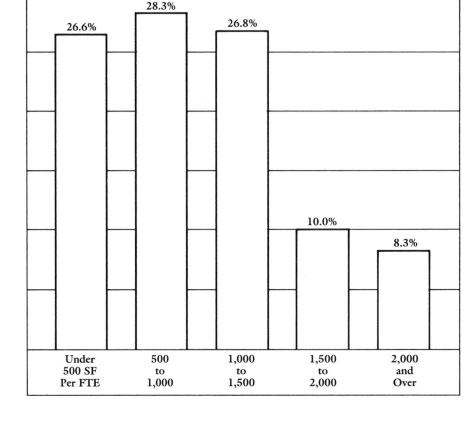

Mean: 990.2

Median: 901.6

Another way of looking at space utilization is to apply the average space utilization for schools of theology to APPA space guidelines for colleges and universities in general, shown in the next chart.

Space Standards

Auxiliary: 10 Percent of Assigned Total Space

Assigned Space Ratio to Total Space: 60 Percent

Source: Rex O. Dillow, ed., *Facilities Management: A Manual for Plant Administration*, second edition.

CLASSROOM:	80 Square Feet Per Student (20 Student Average × 15 Credit Hours at 60 Percent Occupancy)
OFFICE:	150 Square Feet Per Faculty/Staff or 30 Square Feet Per Student (1 Faculty, 2 Staff Per 15 Students)
DORM:	180-220 Square Feet Per Occupant
LIBRARY:	(A) Stack = 1 Square Foot Per 20 Volumes (B) Study = 30 Square Feet × 20 Percent FTE + 10 Percent Faculty (C) Service = 20 Percent of (A) + (B)

It should be noted that although the average of theological schools is comparable to the APPA space guidelines, it also means that half of the institutions have less space and half have more. This phenomenon invites further review by individual institutions. Some schools with space well above average are considering "moth-balling" or even demolishing deteriorated buildings as an effective strategy to bring operating costs and funding needs into a realistic alignment with space needs.

Facilities Operating Budgets

While not an absolute predictor of the extent of CRDM needs, operating budgets for facilities can have a relationship to the extent of backlogs. The two charts on the next page reflect our findings in this area.

Here is how the facilities operating budgets of theological education institutions compare with APPA's data on liberal arts colleges with less than 1,000 FTE:

	Avg. $/Square Foot
Liberal arts colleges under 1,000 FTE	$3.644
(fuel and utilities portion)	0.727*
Schools of theology	2.59
(fuel and utilities portion)	1.12*

*Where electricity is primary or exclusive fuel source

One of the most important findings of this report is that energy efficiency and conservation could release significant *existing funds* to reinvest in plant maintenance. Comments from evaluators in the next chapter offer further evidence of this potential gain for many institutions.

The extensive use of students to perform custodial work at many schools of theology suggests that even in model conditions, the averages in this area will be below comparable costs for small colleges as a whole. The APPA average for utilities is $0.727 per square foot.

What Share of Gross Institutional Expenditure Is Directed to Facilities Operations?

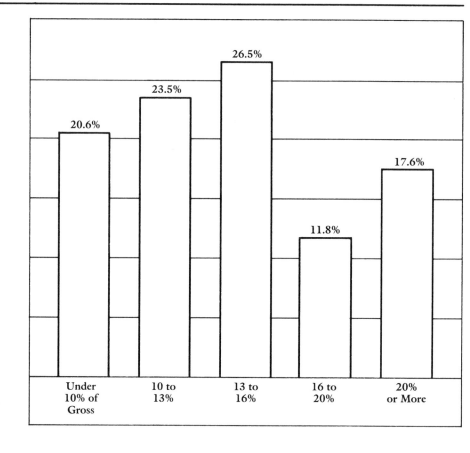

Mean: 13.8%
Median: 13.7%
Average Expenditure: $417,527

Do Ratios of Facilities Expenditures to Annual Gross Institutional Expenditure Have an Effect on Facilities Conditions?

The following shows the average ratio of facilities expenditures to gross institutional expenditure according to FCI.

5.0 or less	5 to 10	8 to 10	10 to 12	12 to 15	15 to 20	20 or more
13.6%	16.4%	15.1%	15.7%	15.1%	15.2%	14.3%

The above data reflects *no* clear relationship between the share of annual expenditures directed to facilities operations (and utilities). However, analysis of this relationship did include:

- Some schools with 2,000 or more square feet per FTE student who were spending over 20 percent of their annual gross expenditure had a "poor" FCI.
- Some schools with under 500 square feet per FTE student who were spending less than 10 percent of their annual gross expenditure had a "good" FCI.

Summary of Findings

- Facilities represent 37,804,098 square feet of campus space at 202 theological schools in the United States and Canada.

- Facilities represent the largest capital asset at schools of theology, with a replacement value of $3.5 billion. This asset is at risk from a documented backlog of $385,173,600 in capital renewal and deferred maintenance needs.

- Most schools of theology are rated in the mid-range by FCI, neither "good" nor "poor." This indicates that, although many schools have substantial backlogs of deferred maintenance, prompt corrective action can prevent a serious, even critical deterioration of facilities in the future for most.

- Housing represents nearly 40 percent of the backlog of capital renewal/deferred maintenance at schools of theology.

- Service systems hold the highest priority of need.

- There is a direct relationship between the average age of campus buildings and facilities conditions.

- While many institutions based their assessment of facilities needs upon actual condition audits, some simply relied on staff estimates. The expense of performing a formal audit is more than justified in order to obtain a full and accurate statement of the true condition of the facilities asset.

- Schools with a high ratio of space per student are also the most likely to have a "poor" facilities condition.

- No evidence links facilities conditions with the share of gross institutional expenditures directed to facilities operations.

- Improved energy efficiency and conservation can release funds from existing expenditures to reinvest in plant operations and staffing.

- Academic priorities, space utilization, level of funding for facilities operations—all are elements that contribute to a comprehensive, long-range plan to correct facilities deterioration and guarantee that the institution can carry out its mission for generations to come.

- A total of sixty-seven institutions, or 33.2 percent of the universe, participated in the research study.

WALTER A. SCHAW

More Than Numbers: A Visit to the Campus

"What would be the most beneficial to me if I was a senior administrator on the staff? . . . What would be my needs, my priorities, my concerns, my programs?"
(An APPA evaluator)

One of the goals of this research project was to evaluate facilities conditions at the forty-one originally selected institutions through a series of on-site visits by APPA member expert evaluators. We believed that, given a common context for such visits, we would better appreciate the characteristics and individual needs of these institutions and gain insights into factors of primary significance.

Planned as a highly interactive two-day site inspection, these visits were not intended to produce judgments or arrive at absolutes. Rather, they were intended to offer observations to enrich the quantitative findings reported in Chapter 1, as well as provide immediate practical benefits to the participating schools.

The expert evaluators were selected on the basis of professional competencies as chief facilities officers with comprehensive experience in the field. While not an expressed objective, we did envision an ongoing and informal support relationship between the evaluators and clients. This relationship has in fact developed as a benefit of the project.

At the end of the site visit, each evaluator submitted a formal report to APPA for review and then to the institution. While the formats varied, each report included the following components:

- Evaluation of general facilities conditions.
- Analysis of staff operations.
- Recommendations on priority facilities needs.
- Appraisal of special conditions, such as age of buildings, ratios of space to students, areas of potential savings, and significant policy issues.

Not included in the formal reports were advice and assistance given on services and contracts available in the local area. Nor did the evaluations of facilities conditions include a thorough, itemized audit of facilities needs, which would have required significantly more time and effort than these visits allowed. Considerable detail, however, was offered concerning any priorities that needed immediate attention—such as water seepage that threatened the foundation of a major building. As a result of this general evaluation, many institutions have arranged to conduct a complete, formal audit of facilities, including a specific definition of funding needs.

The stack of documents produced by the site visits would stand over eight feet high. The following pages present but a sampling of observations common to many reports.

General Observations

A summary of the observations of APPA's evaluators must begin with a recognition of the people having direct responsibility for facilities operations at schools of theology. Comparing this group with small colleges and universities in general, senior administrators and staff at schools of theology are to be commended for doing so much with what, in many instances, is very modest in terms of human resources and funding.

> "The appearance [of the campus] certainly reflects favorably on the efforts of the maintenance department, as it is staffed at a very minimal level and operates on a very austere budget."

> "There is obviously a pride in workmanship and a deep devotion to the institution."

> "The several times I've been on your campus in the last week have left me with a warm feeling that I get when I see something that is receiving loving care."

Throughout the reports, there is evidence of a strong sense of commitment and dedication, from maintenance workers to senior administrators. More than one evaluator expressed that, "I wish I had that dedication in my shop."

An appreciation of stewardship for facilities by the presidents of institutions was reflected in many of the reports.

> "[The president] has a good knowledge of what it takes to create a positive learning environment . . . sound buildings that are conducive to learning and are clean, safe, and aesthetically pleasing. [His] philosophy of facilities is one of understanding and care . . . the dollars spent on buildings were spent wisely."

Given the level of funding, observers often expressed surprise that more critical problems did not exist. But there were significant areas requiring attention, and the balance of this chapter will present comments about the most common and critical of these needs.

Critical Needs

One way to review facilities is by the three types of facilities components: primary structure (foundations, building exteriors, and floor and roof systems); secondary structure (ceilings, walls, windows, and doors); and service systems (heating, cooling, plumbing, electrical, and conveying).

Primary Structure

The largest facilities investment (and therefore the largest potential expense) is in the primary structure—the "brick and mortar." One of the critical points of structural soundness concerns the prevention of water penetration and its subsequent damage. Any weakness in the roof, flashing, or foundation will be revealed by the remorseless working of water.

At more than one institution, evaluators investigated pools of water and found serious problems of runoff and underground water that threatened the foundations of otherwise sound buildings.

> "The problem of surface drainage around the building in general and the specific problem of water coming into the library lower level are significant. A suggestion for the general condition is to have the ground immediately adjacent to the building regraded to restore the proper slope. In several areas, the ground has settled so that the surface water runs to the building foundation rather than away."

> "The apparent settling of the south side of the library should be investigated thoroughly. I believe that the major cause is the lack of gutters and downspouts to divert the rainwater away from the foundation."

Another critical area that threatens the life and usefulness of building structures is the condition of roofs. The APPA evaluators gave practical advice on the care of roofs, repeatedly suggesting that roofing and drainage be addressed as a work priority before performing other, more visible work such as interior repairs and upgrades.

Secondary Structures

Window systems were mentioned in a number of reports as an area for improvement. Window sealing, double panes, and other energy-saving measures are proven to prevent heating and cooling loss, and thus provide a positive return on investment.

Said one report, "The area which requires the most attention and that which will provide the fastest economic return are the window systems."

Service Systems

The physical plant service systems are the "engine" providing essential heat, light, electricity, and water. As illustrated in Chapter 1, most institutions ranked service systems as their most critical facilities need. This point was verified during the campus visits, the evaluators repeatedly citing boilers and power plants as the single most critical need.

Some campuses that appeared attractive and well maintained were being supported by mechanical equipment more than fifty years old (one system dated to 1912). Modifications to original equipment over time had created power plants that were extremely inefficient and at continual risk of breakdown—a definite risk to the academic cycle.

> "Examination of the existing power plant indicated only one boiler being used to heat the entire campus. All of the boilers are older, circa 1925, and approaching the end of their useful life."

> "The solution is to replace the entire system by demolishing and removing the existing cast iron boiler and install two package boilers . . . Presently this dinosaur is loafing and eating up institutional dollars."

Another service system concern in older buildings was the condition of electrical wiring. One report recommended that an entire building be rewired for safety reasons, as well as for convenience of the occupants.

Concerns about humidity controls, particularly for library environments, appeared in several reports.

> "Complaints of extreme humidity were checked . . . no return air grills had been installed in the major portion of the complaint area."

> "The rare book section of the library is in a basement room with no temperature or humidity control. There is an ejector pump located in this room and many overhead drain lines which present potential problems."

Our pernicious friend, water, also showed up in concerns for humidity at one library. One evaluator gave dramatic evidence of how a major problem can develop:

> "The use of a circular sheet metal duct that was installed below the floor as a return air system poses a serious problem. The library's director had mentioned that this duct system, which better serves as a perimeter drain, has filled with water and it was necessary at one time to pump out over 30,000 gallons of water from this subterranean chamber. The idea of water being present in an air duct is not acceptable, particularly in a library operation where humidity is a major concern."

Although service systems may be out of sight, they represent a critical and potentially costly aspect of facilities priorities.

Safety Standards

As a critical need, those components that pose a risk to human health and safety hold a priority of their own. Some reports reflected serious problems.

> "The building is an accident waiting to happen. Besides the electrical system and stairs mentioned earlier, various hazardous substances are improperly stored . . . high hazard operations such as welding and gasoline engine maintenance are conducted without proper ventilation and fire protection. There are two CO_2 extinguishers in the building, both last inspected in 1970. By affording a false sense of security, they are probably worse than no extinguishers at all since they almost surely are discharged."

> "Fire extinguishers are too few, of the wrong type, and long overdue for inspection . . . the distance-to-exit criteria aren't met . . . stair risers are of varying height on both interior stairs and outdoor fire escapes . . . only the library area is equipped with smoke and heat detectors and an alarm system."

At some institutions, a major investment has been made to ensure human health and safety, as well as environmental issues. One school spent nearly $2 million to perform renovations to comply with state and local life safety codes. The measures included providing access to persons with disabilities, retrofitting PBC transformers, and encapsulating asbestos.

But not every corrective recommendation requires an expenditure:

> "The basement of the dorms are at present a fire hazard. The residents have dumped many possessions with little regard for order. Charcoal grills are among the piles. This area should be cleaned up quickly!"

Functionality of Buildings

The roof may not need repair and service systems may be in good order, but the building may not satisfy the functional requirements of the institution. At some schools, for example, dormitories constructed for young, single students now need to serve a growing population of older, married students.

Access for people with disabilities appeared in some reports as an issue of functionality. One observer simply said of one campus that it is "not accessible to the physically disabled. Ramps are very few and of the wrong slope. Classrooms are not at all accessible."

Not surprisingly, the age of buildings had a direct relationship to their functionality, and some campuses enjoyed the advantages of more recent construction:

> "Because many of the buildings are relatively new, they are well suited to their usage. The new classroom building, with upgraded classrooms and offices, brings the campus to first class quality."

Space Utilization

The community of institutions examined in this study reflects a wide range of existing space in proportion to student populations, as discussed in Chapter 1. Despite the substantial overall growth in enrollments for theological schools in the past twenty-five years (26,000 in 1956 to 56,000 today), some older, large institutions have space-to-students ratios that stretch their financial resources and consequently their ability to adequately maintain existing buildings.

Other institutions operate at a much lower ratio of space to students. Newness of the institution and rapid growth are factors where space may still be catching up.

General observations about space need to be qualified by factors such as students' residency, type of housing (married or single), size of library collections, and other special factors that may be unique to a campus and the institution's mission. Observers were surprised at the space given to libraries in proportion to the size of the collections, until they learned that many libraries at theological schools serve as a denominational resource as well.

Evaluator reports on schools with a sizeable space-to-students ratio included comments such as: "All facilities are underused, including the classrooms and chapel. The dining area and kitchen are seldom used." And at the other end of the spectrum: "Five of seven major facilities concerns identified by your institution relate to insufficient space . . . All of these areas seem to be legitimate problems."

Some reports included corrective actions for improved space utilization. Typical was a suggestion that a classroom be made more flexible by dividing it in two with a folding partition and adding doors.

Campus Appearance

Many evaluators gave high praise to institutions for the appearance of their campuses.

> "The campus has twelve buildings that are generally older but well maintained considering the funds dedicated to this task. The

condition of the campus is particularly noteworthy considering that all of the maintenance, custodial, and operational work is performed by two full-time personnel."

"Grounds and interior maintenance were noted to be excellent. Although janitorial staffing initially appeared to be low based on square footage of occupied space, traffic in buildings is extremely light and the population well disciplined. I wish I had the same situation!"

On the other hand, some APPA evaluators noted that a good appearance may hide some serious problems.

"The general appearance of the plant is good, with a pleasing modern architectural image on a well-planned site, appropriately supported with landscape . . . A second more detailed look does expose some serious unfunded facility deficiencies which will continue to increase exponentially if not addressed in the near term."

A 1985 study conducted by the Carnegie Foundation for the Advancement of Teaching examined the factors most affecting students' college choices. The impression of the buildings and grounds based on a campus visit was cited as the most important factor by well over half of the students in that study. While prospective students at schools of theology may be motivated differently than the general student population, a pleasant place to live and learn still helps to attract students, as one evaluator pointed out:

"Improving the secondary structure is not the highest priority. However, it would improve morale, be attractive to students, staff, administration, and faculty, and make an atmosphere that is more conducive to learning and working."

Generally, schools of theology tend to have an attractive environment despite budgets that were often referred to in the reports as "austere." The dedication of staff was clearly responsible for the appearance of many campuses.

Maintenance and Operations

While housekeeping and custodial tasks were being carried out with generally good results in terms of appearance, campus evaluators pointed out a need for more formal maintenance programs at many institutions. Many of the reports underscored the importance of preventive maintenance, routine inspection of facilities, and servicing of mechanical systems as critical in preventing the accumulation of additional deferred maintenance.

"There are 3.5 physical plant employees. The size of the staff looks to be adequate for the facility. However, there is no formal maintenance program. Initiation of a preventive maintenance program is strongly recommended."

"A formal work management/preventive maintenance program should be established to assure that tasks are completed and proper identification of work backlogs is made. Without proper data, any request for additional resources is futile."

Many suggestions emerged from the evaluators in this area. Some recommended consideration of outside contractors to supplement existing staffs and provide technical expertise. Others suggested that senior staff members cross train others. One evaluator recommended training to ensure that more than one person is knowledgeable in the different trades in order to provide depth. Still others recommended computerization as a means of incorporating special knowledge and experience.

While outside contractors were recommended for support roles in a number of evaluation reports, some caveats were issued:

"An effective preventive maintenance program can have real benefits in extending equipment life and eliminating unnecessary breakdowns. However, the seminary is relying on the current vendor to ensure that they have a cost-effective program. There is a basic incompatibility of interests in having the contractor set the requirements, perform the work, and evaluate the effectiveness of the PM program. The seminary should obtain the services of a consultant to monitor performance."

"The seminary has relied completely on the word of the contractor to establish these requirements and relies totally on the integrity of the contract to perform the required work. There is no independent validation of the contractor's performance."

Several institutions have mixed in-house and contract services with excellent results, as long as the contractors have been independently monitored.

Other Staffing Observations

Many institutions were able to achieve high quality with low costs by utilizing students for custodial and grounds maintenance. One critical factor did appear when comparing institutions in this area: those paying higher wages tended to have much less turnover than those paying the minimum wage. The difference in quality and dependable performance was clear in the evaluators' reports:

"Salaries for student workers are too low for some to work in physical plant without creating hardship on them or their families. Efforts to raise the wage rate in incremental fashion will be done as soon as possible."

"Student wages have now been raised. This has been influential in stabilizing the work force. This has also been a helpful recruiting tool for especially skilled laborers, since there are few jobs which pay in this range that allow a flexibility of hours."

One observer of a school with excellent student help addressed the need for skilled staff as well:

> "While very effective at what they do with student labor, I would like to see another professional staff member versed in the HVAC trade to make conservation efforts stay in place. This person would be a major contributor to the preventive maintenance programs."

Time spent by facilities managers on tasks other than managing was pointed out by a number of evaluators as another area for review. One evaluator noted that "the plant director spends most of his time as a maintenance mechanic, leaving little time to properly plan operations and manage."

Energy Conservation

Energy costs at schools of theology were compared with those costs at APPA member colleges of 1,000 FTE or less. With this one important exception, the schools of theology spent far less than the APPA average; the exception was in the cost per square foot per year for fuel and utilities. As discussed earlier in this chapter, antiquated boilers and other equipment in dire need of replacement represent one of the primary causes for the higher utilities expense.

While not characteristic of most schools of theology, some institutions showed serious deficiencies in this area. One evaluator commented: "Almost every piece of mechanical equipment on campus was either inoperable, inadequately repaired, or so neglected that inefficient use of utilities was the norm."

A number of reports included estimates of cost savings from implementing more efficient mechanical systems.

> "Present methods of controlling humidity through electric reheat coils are very costly to maintain. Electric energy costs could be reduced by approximately two-thirds if steam reheat were provided. The cost of these modifications is approximately $55,000. The savings in electric heat costs would be approximately $11,800 annually."

A common recommendation called on institutions to conduct energy audits, review rate schedules, and work more closely with their local utilities.

> "The utility company can put on a portable demand chart recorder on any incoming power line and monitor the electrical usage for one week. This service should be free. With the recorder information, the school can then evaluate the economical savings of load shedding and time clocks."

> "With an annual energy bill between $300,000 and $400,000, it would be prudent to have detailed energy audits completed again and an institution-wide energy conservation program expanded.

Such a program could yield 10 percent or more savings on the energy bill."

Again, not every suggestion required a major outlay. Much of the advice was simple and highly practical.

"Many techniques exist to keep a place bright and not burn excessive energy. Pick good reflective colors for paints and wall coverings. Adjust the time of day functions as daylight increases; shed electrical loads as workers depart. Keep all equipment on your duty cycle with timed night setbacks. Optimize equipment functions by buying the right size for the load. You'll get more heat or cooling from fan coils that are routinely cleaned and maintained."

The human equation was reflected in more than one comment by evaluators. One wrote: "The system is either out of balance or one of the tenants has an unusual need for warmth. My suspicions are toward the latter. Room temperatures should be checked. If they are uniformly overheated, the tenants should be asked to tolerate lower temperatures."

Planning

How can the various facilities needs, reported by the APPA evaluators and later defined in detail by audits, be integrated into a set of priorities for available and future funds? The evaluators were asked to give their views on this in their written reports. In many instances, reports of current and planned activity put an optimistic outlook to what may have otherwise appeared as an awesome list of critical needs.

"The seminary has implemented effective financial plans for these new buildings to avoid future financial problems. These were paid for and endowed before they were built. They were built with high quality standards and have minimized long-term maintenance requirements."

Others recommended the integration of facilities needs into existing plans.

"Thought should be given to link the physical plant maintenance department to the seminary's mission through a specific set of goals and objectives. This process can help students, faculty, and administration identify and define priorities and delegate responsibilities in a way that is accepted and understood."

"In reviewing the strategic long-range plan, questions need to be answered with respect to what facilities will be required if the student body is to increase. Also, what will be required if the library collection is to be strengthened? What facilities will be required for each new program?"

Conclusion

The intent of this chapter was to provide insights into facilities issues through the selected comments of the forty-one APPA evaluators. In general, the evaluators found schools of theology to be in better condition than they had expected, considering the costs for staffing and operations at other institutions of comparable size. This opinion is validated by the quantitative data from research reported in Chapter 1.

WALTER A. SCHAW

Audits and Equilibrium

"There are no magic answers . . . there is no tooth fairy that funds facilities, either new construction or renovation." (Ford, 1990)

Although facilities represent the largest capital asset of most institutions of higher education, prior to the publication of *The Decaying American Campus: A Ticking Time Bomb* (Rush, 1989), many colleges and universities did not have an accurate view of the true condition of that asset. Also lacking was a conceptual language to translate facilities needs into a financial model that would treat facilities as any other asset, preserving its capacity to perform its function over the long term.

In the past few years, a conceptual model has been introduced and widely adopted, not only by individual institutions but by state higher education commissions and others. This "facilities equilibrium" model ensures the long-term investment in facilities by treating this asset as a portfolio of investments. A similar strategy traditionally has been used in the preservation of cash endowments.

There are four essential steps in the management of an institution's facilities as a portfolio (Rush, 1991):

1. *Establish meaningful baseline data* about facilities conditions through a detailed, structured inspection process.

2. *Establish short- and long-range renewal needs* using the data obtained from the facility inspection.

3. *Create decision-support models* to calculate alternate reinvestment rates and the effect those rates have on short- and long-term facility conditions.

4. *Report on the facilities portfolio* to governing boards, senior management, and managers responsible for maintaining the facilities portfolio.

This chapter reviews the first two elements as they relate to our experience with schools of theology. The last two elements are addressed in subsequent chapters of this report.

The Facilities Condition Audit

A facilities condition audit is the identification, inspection, and condition assessment in a building-by-building analysis with information organized in a manner that supports planning and decision-making. The baseline data derived from this audit is an essential first step in planning, funding, and implementing an effective management strategy.

At the onset of the APPA/Lilly project in 1990, the original forty-one participating institutions were asked for basic information about the extent of facilities and their condition. Most respondents displayed a good grasp of the general composition of their campuses—the number of buildings, building ages, and total square footage. Most also appeared to have only estimates of the condition of those buildings, although several schools had conducted partial or complete inspection audits.

In the several workshops conducted for the pilot group, the importance of performing thorough facilities audits was stressed. As a result, most of the schools in the pilot group have initiated either general audits or audits directed to specific priority needs.

The initial survey also established a data base of standard elements, such as square footage and functional use of buildings, that has been retained in an ongoing reference file for theological institutions in the United States and Canada. A second survey, forwarded to all 202 schools in early 1991, expanded the data to include a more complete universe of theological schools.

Initial Assessment

The facilities inspection process is a visual inspection of all structural and mechanical components of each facility. Safety needs such as asbestos identification, as well as functional requirements such as access for people with disabilities, are commonly within the scope of a formal facilities inspection. The inspectors—whether in-house staff or outside contractors—are trained to give a systematic, comprehensive evaluation that includes a reasonable estimate of cost for correction and the identification of priorities over time.

In our study, we found that many schools with small staffs contracted with outside firms who were experienced and qualified to conduct facilities condition audits. In many instances, the contracting firms trained in-house staff to perform periodic audits after their work was complete. Institution staffs were equipped with modest but effective computer programs to maintain information on building conditions in a consistent, ongoing program of inspection. The APPA/Lilly workshops stressed the need for regular inspection, along with preventive maintenance programs, to ensure that unexpected backlogs of capital replacement would not develop in the future.

Setting Priorities

One of the most valuable contributions of a facilities condition audit is to establish priorities for CRDM needs. These priorities are reviewed with the institution prior to a final audit report so that the assessment of building conditions can be linked with the priorities of the institution's mission and strategic plan.

A high-priority condition is one that, if further neglected, will pose a substantially greater cost in the future. An example is the timely repair of a roof: delay in this critical area may result in the much more expensive replacement of the roof or, worse, cause damage to the primary structure.

Another high-priority item is any correction to ensure life safety. Some of these, like asbestos removal, are regulated activites that carry the hazard of penalties for noncompliance.

Few institutions—whether schools of theology or large research universities—have the funding capacity to correct all their CRDM needs, even the high priorities. Many of the formal audit programs present a schedule of needs over a period from five to ten years with annual funding levels established.

In the following pages, excerpts from actual audits performed at schools of theology are presented to illustrate the different styles of reports and types of information produced by audits.

The Assessment Summary reports are provided to reflect the same total requirements in maintenance and repair costs sorted by various categories, and to provide ratio averages involving current replacement values, age, gross square feet, and total cost of deficiencies as a common denominator.

1991 BUILDING CONDITION ASSESSMENT

NUMBER OF FACILITIES	12
GROSS SQUARE FOOTAGE *	109,275 SF
AVERAGE AGE *	47 YEARS
CURRENT PLANT VALUE *	$8,061,328
TEN YEAR REQUIREMENT	$1,783,874
YEAR ONE REQUIREMENT	$ 91,330

*(Includes ten buildings, no data on misc. facilities)

TEN YEAR MAINTENANCE AND REPAIR PLAN

The Ten Year Maintenance and Repair Plan is a report that lists by facility each deficiency with the recommended priority. Ten priorities were used for the Seminary which translate into a ten year plan. All costs are expressed in 1991 dollar amounts.

YEAR 1 - $ 91,330
YEAR 2 - $641,352
YEAR 3 - $348,879
YEAR 4 - $ 58,911
YEAR 5 - $413,931
YEAR 6 - $121,077
YEAR 7 - $ 23,424
YEAR 8 - $ 5,786
YEAR 9 - $ 10,658
YEAR 10 - $ 68,525

04/22/91

PAGE 1

FACILITY COMPONENT COST SUMMARY
ALL COMPONENTS
SORT BY SYSTEM

SYSTEM	Y0/1 1991/92	Y2 1993	Y3 1994	Y4 1995	Y5 1996	TOTAL
A PRIMARY STRUCTURES						
00 MISCELLANEOUS INFRASTRUCTURES	900	29,613	0	255	0	30,768
01 FOUNDATION SYSTEM	0	0	0	0	0	0
02 COLUMN & EXTERIOR WALL SYSTEM	11,697	24,922	4,300	2,010	92	43,021
03 FLOOR SYSTEM	43	0	0	0	0	43
04 ROOF	44,220	33,242	76,350	1,350	0	155,162
05 OTHER PRIMARY STRUCTURES	1,990	9,618	964	50	0	12,622
B SECONDARY STRUCTURES						
06 CEILING SYSTEM	2,024	6,000	6,742	0	0	14,766
07 FLOOR COVERING	0	36,132	9,322	45,688	30,829	121,971
08 INT WALLS & PARTITION SYSTEM	2,554	31,672	10,081	5,096	35,333	84,738
09 STAIRWAYS	2,400	0	15,000	0	0	17,400
10 WINDOW SYSTEM	5,354	39,936	94,823	495	70,704	211,312
11 DOOR SYSTEM	1,979	15,986	2,801	294	33,625	54,685
C SERVICE SYSTEMS						
12 COOLING	236	15,823	65,019	0	37,835	118,914
13 HEATING	0	80,320	37,626	2,369	1,788	122,103
14 VENTILATING	3,725	7,563	145	0	530	11,963
15 ELECTRICAL-SERVICE & DISTRIBUTION	308	0	6,979	0	16,494	23,781
16 ELECTRICAL-LIGHTING & POWER	10,123	87,713	11,561	0	17,262	126,659
17 ELECTRICAL-SPECIAL SYSTEMS	1,736	0	0	0	0	1,736
18 PLUMBING	957	151,141	4,365	1,303	70,439	228,206
19 EXTINGUISHING SYSTEMS	0	0	0	0	0	0
20 ELEVATORS	0	0	0	0	0	0
21 OTHER SERVICE SYSTEMS	1,083	71,670	2,800	0	99,000	174,553
TOTAL	91,330	641,352	348,879	58,911	413,931	1,554,404

SUMMARY - DEFERRED MAINTENANCE
Lounges/Dormitory Building

Action	Cat.	Estimate
Replace single phase feeders with three phase feeders.	III	$ 5,300
Replace single phase panels with three phase panels.	III	$ 12,000
Split each service into a lighting circuit and a receptacle circuit and add receptacles.	III	$ 21,000
Remove and replace cracked windows.	III	$ 5,800
Replace exterior door hardware.	III	$ 35,000
Replace closers.	III	$ 5,500
Incorporate key card system.	III	$ 10,000
TOTAL - III		**$273,000**
Remove 1 x 1 tile from ceilings and replace with lay-in panels.	IV	$ 15,000
Investigate life safety code compliance.	IV	$ 5,000
Remove 1 x 1 tiles from walls and patch plaster.	IV	$ 25,000
Investigate means of egress.	IV	$ 1,500
Investigate fire ratings.	IV	$ 2,500
Study handicap accessibility requirements.	IV	$ 4,000
TOTAL - IV		**$ 53,000**
Repair/replace doors and frames.	V	$ 56,500
Seal cracks in basement concrete slab.	V	$ 2,000
Repairing damage and updating corridors and lounges.	V	$105,000

BUILDING PROFILE

Building Name:	Dormitory/Lounges
Building Number:	6
Date:	4/11/91
Contact Name:	
Phone Number:	
Year Occupied:	1923
Initial Cost:	
Function:	Meeting, retreat, classes, reception space. Housing for single students, guest rooms, storage.
Occupants by Department:	90 students maximum with 4 - 2 person guest rooms.
Gross Square Footage:	38,207
Net Usable Square Footage:	

Renovations Description:

	Date:	Cost:
Bathroom and room improvements.		
HVAC installations and replacements, 3rd floor room additions, bathroom improvements, other mechanical systems improvements and additions.	1965	
Refinish of guest room. Redecorating of Lounge.	1977	
Building fire alarm system and individual room smoke detector.	1984	

Summary of Maintenance Records:
Routine maintenance of HVAC systems.
Relamping and fixture repair.
Painting as needed.
Other surface repair or replacement as needed.
Plumbing including drain cleaning, faucet problems, and shower stalls replacement over last 15 years.
Roof and exterior as needed.
Window repair.
Furnishings repair and replacement.

Service Contractor Name: See attached list.	**Address:**	**Contact Person:**
	Telephone Number:	

Facilities Equilibrium

The overall goal of facilities management is to ensure the facilities necessary to fulfill the institution's mission for future generations as well as the present. The concepts involved in achieving facilities equilibrium have been articulated in several publications since 1989 (see in particular Rush, 1991). The maintenance of facilities equilibrium requires a continuous and predictable capital investment based on an objective assessment of existing facility conditions and the long-term goals and objectives of the institution.

The APPA/Lilly workshops presented four essentials to establishing this equilibrium, including the model reproduced on the next page.

1. ***Reduce backlogs*** of capital renewal and deferred maintenance in a schedule of five to ten years (five years is recommended for this "catching up").

2. ***Fund an annual cost of replacement and renewal***, in addition to the reduction of backlogs. This funding recognizes an annual weardown of buildings and equipment during the normal use of the facilities asset. For example, a new building can be assumed to have a lifetime of as much as 100 years. Each year, the average weardown would be 1 percent of its value, a cost that would accumulate to 100 percent if no work were done. (Keep in mind that the annual cost that applies here is the replacement cost, not the value of the original construction.)

Replacement and renewal funding must also recognize the value of all of the components that allow the building to function. Roofs, heating and air conditioning systems, electrical systems, windows, and interior walls—each of these components has a predictable average lifetime that must be calculated into a realistic projection of annual funding for replacement and renewal.

The SCUP/APPA/NACUBO model proposes an annual renewal and replacement fund of 1.5 to 3.5 percent of replacement cost. The low end of that range may suffice for a campus with relatively new, well-constructed buildings; the upper range is appropriate for large research institutions. Given APPA's experience with small colleges, we recommend that annual funding for schools of theology be established at *2 percent of replacement value of all buildings*.

It should be noted that the actual application of replacement and renewal funds will follow a pattern of "spikes"—costs in some years will exceed and in other years fall below the annual fund allocation. For this reason, it is important that the

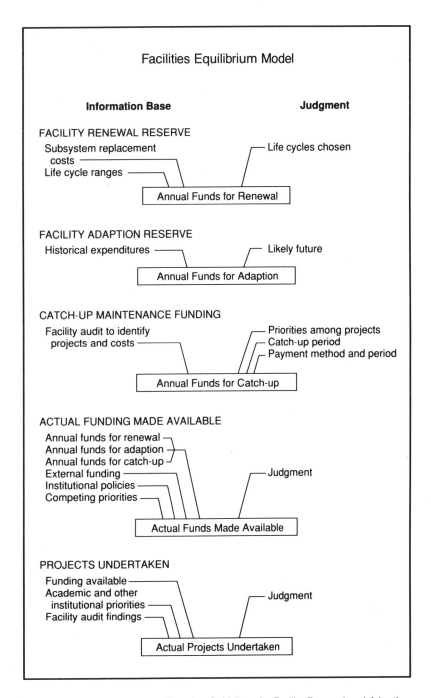

Source: John A. Dunn Jr., *Financial Planning Guidelines for Facility Renewal and Adaption*

replacement and renewal fund be treated as a reserve and allowed to accumulate.

By way of illustration, the component life of a heating and ventilation system may be fifteen years. Continuous preventive maintenance may extend its life, and funds for replacement may not be used until year eighteen. In the meantime, however, two roofs that were supposed to last twenty years may need extensive repair after only fifteen.

We recommend at least three years of experience with funding this reserve before adjusting the annual rate, and in no instance should the initial rate be less than 1.5 percent of replacement value. Just as one cannot momentarily observe a tree growing, so it is impossible to witness the ongoing weardown of buildings and their components. But it is important to recognize that building and component use is an actual annual cost to be funded.

One final word of caution: funding for CRDM backlogs must be kept separate from capital renewal and replacement funding in order to achieve facilities equilibrium. The renewal fund simply maintains the facility in its present condition, however good or poor that condition may be.

3. *Adaption* is the third essential component of facilities equilibrium presented in the model. The roof may not leak and its renewal may be funded, but equilibrium is not achieved if the building it serves does not function adequately for its present purpose.

Adaption is the "wild card" in financial planning for full facilities equilibrium. An example of the purpose of an adaption allowance is a dormitory that is structurally sound but constructed for single students may prove inadequate for married couples. Regulatory compliance is another function of the adaption component.

Funds required to reduce backlogs and address annual renewal and replacement can be projected quite accurately, especially once a facilities audit is performed. Adaption provides the extra margin for ensuring a long-term, effective financial plan.

It may be helpful to illustrate the financial planning model by applying the formula to a typical school of theology:

Total square feet of facilities:	174,450
Replacement value (at $93 per square foot)	$16,223,850
Audited backlog of CRDM	1,617,151

Applying the guidelines to an annual appropriation:

1. Reduction of CRDM backlog (seven-year schedule, plus adjustments) — $250,000

2. Plant reserve for renewal and replacement (2 percent of replacement value) — 324,500

3. Allowance for average annual adaption costs   81,100

4. Annual budget for plant operations
   (at $3.05 per square foot, including fuel)   532,072

Annual funding required to achieve
facilities equilibrium $1,187,672

Kriemelmeyer Curve of Inevitable Consequences

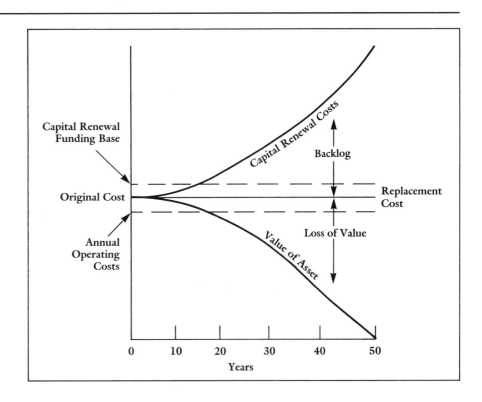

Source: Harry Kriemelmeyer Jr., in remarks to APPA Institute for Facilities Finance, November 19, 1991.

The illustration above begins at the midpoint, with the initial cost of construction. This midpoint is adjusted annually to reflect the true cost of replacement. Just below the midpoint is a level cost of operations (maintenance, cleaning, minor repairs). Neglect of this function can negatively affect the continuing value of the asset. Performing this function, however, does not assure the value of the asset unless funding is also provided for major capital renewal and replacement (roofs, service systems, etc.).

Just above the midpoint is the annual renewal and replacement investment (2 percent per year) for a typical building. Little or no cost is incurred during the first few years, but costs begin to escalate as the building ages. Failure to fund and apply renewal allowances creates deferred maintenance.

The lower curve is in direct proportion to the upper curve. When the cost of deficiencies is equal to the cost of replacement, the asset has been entirely used up—the inevitable consequence.

Conclusion

This chapter reviewed the essentials of managing the facilities asset as presented in the APPA/Lilly workshop series for the forty-one schools who participated in the original project. A first step for any school in managing its facilities asset is to develop baseline information about the size and condition of campus facilities. For many schools, especially those with older buildings and some degree of deterioration, a condition audit is recommended before a true appraisal and financial plan are possible.

Even with the most comprehensive financial planning, the components of staffing and operations also play an essential role. The comments of APPA evaluators in Chapter 2 illustrate that failure to systematically manage work and conduct periodic preventive maintenance can have a significant adverse effect on future facilities conditions and projections of expenditures.

The reduction of existing deferred maintenance alone does not guarantee that future backlogs will not occur. This requires annual funding for renewal that considers the annual weardown of structures and support systems, and anticipates changes in function and the potential cost of government regulation. A balanced approach will help achieve the goal of facilities equilibrium, preserving and enhancing the facilities investment for future generations of students.

JOSEPH P. O'NEILL

Financing for Renewal and Replacement

One clear message did emerge . . . Congregations did not lessen their charitable giving, but they gave to causes that were sharply defined.

When stripped to its essentials, the concept of financing is based on three legal ways of getting money: you can earn it, you can borrow it, or you can persuade someone to give it to you. All other financing vehicles are derivatives or combinations of these three basic modes.

Earning and borrowing are reciprocals of each other. You can't borrow unless you can show that you can earn enough to pay it back with interest. Earning and borrowing imply a direct quid pro quo: my labor in return for compensation; my money in return for a fixed interest or a share of the profits.

Gifts are another matter. Some, like free-will offerings to disaster victims, involve no quid pro quo at all. But gifts to colleges, hospitals, and schools of theology are not usually of this nature. They are more like implicit contracts or third-party payments. They imply an indirect quid pro quo: my money, not with a return for myself, but to benefit a worthy activity or person. In other words, charitable institutions ordinarily earn their gifts by the services they perform.

The basic fact about most theological schools is that they earn so little from tuition and fees that they need to earn far more from gifts than any other sector of higher education. According to data from the Association of Theological Schools (ATS), in 1989-90, student tuition and fees covered less than a quarter of the average theological school's operating budget. If this revenue figure were computed net of tuition discounts, the percentage of seminary costs covered by tuition and fees would be closer to 15 percent. In 1989-90, the list price of tuition at the 202 seminaries accredited by the ATS averaged $3,600 per year while the actual cost per full-time equivalent (FTE) student was $16,020.

One serious consequence of this tuition and fee structure is that most seminary facilities are not self-amortizing. That is, users' fees are so low that they cannot be relied upon as a sole source to recover the costs of financing a new facility. Indeed, in 1990 the average per-student tuition at schools of theology, net of tuition discounts, barely covered the average maintenance and operating costs of approximately $2,300 per FTE student. As a result, about one-third of the forty-one seminaries and divinity schools invited to participate in the APPA/Lilly project were in the "fair-to-poor" or "poor" category when the state of their physical facilities was evaluated. The current tuition structure does not allow them to retain enough earnings to maintain their physical plant.

Why are tuition and fees so low? The tradition of very low or no tuition for students of theology was first established at Andover, the earliest of the Protestant seminary foundations. Like cadets at West Point, where education has always been free, candidates for ordained ministry are considered initiates in a corporate structure within which, in due time, they will become full members. Just as General Motors does not charge employees for on-the-job training, in most denominations, the church at large—national, regional, and local—makes itself responsible for most or even all of the costs of a theological education.

For example, as a matter of policy, the seminaries of the Southern Baptist Convention do not charge tuition. The denomination collects funds nationally from individuals and local congregations and then distributes these monies to SBC seminaries. In the United Methodist Church, local congregations are urged to contribute 2 percent of their net disposable income toward the support of seminaries. The Presbyterian and Episcopal Churches have adopted plans similar to that of the Methodist Church, but with a suggested 1 percent contribution from local congregations. In the Roman Catholic Church, a diocese usually levies a "tax" on each parish, part of which goes to the support of students for the priesthood.

The funds so collected are usually disbursed according to some formula that guarantees an equitable distribution among a denomination's several seminaries. But these formulas apply only to operating, not capital, budgets. That is, the distribution formulas are tied to such operating criteria as current enrollment or the number of graduates who enter the parish ministry.

The funding formulas ignore the needs of capital renewal. No part of any current denominational funding formula takes account of square footage or age of facilities. As a result, theological schools are almost entirely dependent upon free-will gifts to reduce their backlog of deferred maintenance.

Theological schools and their sponsoring denominations need to reexamine the ways they fund their capital needs. Under current practice, many denominations require a seminary to ask permission to conduct a capital campaign. But once permission is received, the school is on its own and collects what it can for its own internal use. This type of laissez-faire system may make some sense for new construction, since it allows the "market" (i.e., the willingness of donors to contribute to a particular project) to determine whether a new building will be built. But as a way to keep existing structures in good repair, a laissez-faire system of raising capital makes very little sense at all.

The need for capital renewal is marked both by its predictability and its inevitability. From the moment a new building is opened, its structure and systems begin to deteriorate at well-known and easily calculated rates. Roofs must be replaced in twenty-five to thirty years; elevators and heating systems have useful lives of fifteen to twenty years; road systems begin to go after twenty years. A denomination cannot afford to let its investment in facilities be lost when one of its schools is unable or too inept to obtain enough capital to maintain the integrity of its buildings and facilities.

A laissez-faire approach to the financing of capital renewal has two significant drawbacks: 1) the institutions that can raise the most money are not necessarily the most in need of it; and 2) the deterioration of physical facilities is inexorable. Delays only increase the cost of repair and may result in a crisis that wipes out previous investment. For many schools of theology, gifts are too uncertain, loans too expensive, and an increase in tuition and fees too unrealistic to be considered reliable sources for a capital renewal and replacement program.

It should be noted in passing that when seminaries wish to borrow for capital projects, they labor under more handicaps than any other sector of higher education. The most notable restriction is that, in many states, they are barred from the tax-exempt bond markets. The provisions of some state constitutions against aid to religious institutions are even more restrictive than the First Amendment constraints of the U.S. constitution. When schools of theology borrow in those states, they must do so at a market rate. And paying a market rate of interest, especially in the last decade, would have made most of these projects prohibitively expensive.

One possible approach to deal with financing capital renewal is a denomination-wide campaign to establish a renewal and replacement fund upon which all of the church's seminaries might draw. Such a fund might be used to guarantee loans so that schools, especially those with small endowments, could borrow at lower rates of interest than would ordinarily be available to them. If the fund were of sufficient size, it might be structured as a revolving loan facility that could lend at low interest up to, say, one-third of the annual cost of renewal and replacement. For projects that may be self-funding, such as energy conservation measures, the fund might share in the savings that the school experiences over time.

Energy projects are especially attractive because so many facilities at schools of theology are energy inefficient. According to data provided in Chapter 1 of this report, the average school of theology pays significantly more per square foot for fuel and utilities than the average small liberal arts college. The payback on some energy projects—for example, replacing incandescent with fluorescent lighting—is two years or less. More efficient heating plants or energy-conserving windows have paybacks of five to ten years. Ideally, the savings from energy conservation could be reinvested in other capital renewal projects.

Despite the obvious good sense of maintaining the integrity of the physical plant, there are many barriers to establishing a capital renewal fund. Some are related to church finances in general. Over the past twenty years, most major denominations have seen a decline, at the national level at least, in their ability to raise money. During the rapid inflation of the mid- to late 1970s national church income remained stagnant. And, in most denominations, subsidies to schools of theology fell dramatically in real dollar terms. In 1968, for example, the General Assembly of the United Presbyterian Church provided its seven seminaries with $1,986,811. On average, this covered 22.3 percent of their operating budgets. In 1990, the General Assembly provided eleven seminaries (the number increased due to church merger) with $2,776,000, a sum that covered less than 5 percent of seminary budgets.

As a denomination's support for theological education declines, one can ask whether this is due to a fall in total revenues or whether spending on other priorities has increased. A ten-year study (1977-1986) of the finances of the United Church of Christ showed that the income of local congregations kept pace with inflation. However, local congregations reduced their giving to national church bodies, and an increasing proportion of local church budgets went to current operations. At the local level, most of this shift occurred at the expense of the congregation's capital budget and may, in good part, reflect the fact that as inflation lowers the real cost of debt service, it raises the nominal cost of salaries.

One clear message did emerge from the United Church of Christ study. Congregations did not lessen their charitable giving, but they gave to causes that were sharply defined. A fundraising campaign at the national level, especially if it is focused on the needs of schools, may be a viable fundraising vehicle. As more church money stays at the local level and as national funding decreases, schools of theology have increasingly turned to local congregations as a source of support. But the change is a costly one. Each dollar raised at the local level costs more, due to the expense of fundraising, than one received as a denominational subsidy. New fundraising strategies at the national level should be considered.

Financial problems are not the only barriers to establishing a fund for capital renewal. When a seminary turns to its sponsoring denomination for financial assistance, a certain structural tension is involved that varies from denomination to denomination. Although seminaries are institutions of the church, they are usually independently incorporated and, more importantly, usually strive to maintain a certain academic sovereignty. As a rule of thumb, the greater the academic sovereignty, the lower the support from the denomination. Types of denominational sponsorship range from the almost laissez-faire relationship between the United Church of Christ or the American Baptist Churches and their related seminaries to the controlling interest that the Southern Baptist Convention and the Roman Catholic Church exercise over their centers of theological education. The other major denominations fall in between these two poles, each with varying degrees of support and control.

A capital renewal fund would almost necessarily involve an increase in the level of denominational control. To maintain the viability of its funding base, a revolving loan fund would not ordinarily invest in facilities whose cost of repair would exceed the cost of new construction. Each denomination would have to determine which buildings would be eligible for funding. But given the difficulty of borrowing in the current recessionary environment, a minor loss of independence is a small price to pay for the integrity of physical plant. Capital renewal is too important an issue to be left to chance or the vagaries of the market.

DANIEL CONWAY

CHAPTER 5

Christian Stewardship of Facilities: Looking Ahead in Hope

It may be that the pressing need to disarm the "ticking time bomb" of deferred maintenance will be the occasion for a new working definition of this ancient, and much abused, Christian virtue.

The APPA/Lilly study reveals that, for the most part, theological schools in the United States and Canada have taken good care of their physical facilities. Indeed, given their limited human and financial resources—and the significant changes that have taken place in seminary culture during the past thirty years—the 202 theological schools studied in this project have done a remarkable job of caring for their physical resources.

Yet there remains a serious challenge in the form of an average backlog of $1.9 million in capital renewal and deferred maintenance costs per theological school. How can the average theological school hope to meet this enormous capital need and still maintain its commitment to the overall mission and goals of theological education?

As we look ahead to the next decade and beyond, the challenges that theological schools face in their efforts to preserve and develop their largest capital asset call for a new understanding of stewardship—especially as this concept is related to the development of a seminary's human, physical, and financial resources. In fact, it may be that the pressing need to disarm the "ticking time bomb" of deferred maintenance will be the occasion for a new working definition of this ancient, and much abused, Christian virtue.

Even a cursory glance at contemporary writing on the theology and practice of stewardship reveals widespread agreement that, as applied to the personal stewardship of individual Christians, the popular understanding of this term has degenerated from what was once understood as the totality of a Christian's response to the mystery of God's love to a purely functional description of the duties and obligations of daily Christian living. Some even suggest that stewardship has become little more than a euphemism for fundraising.

John H. Westerhoff III, in *Building God's People in a Materialistic Society*, comments on this devaluation of the concept of stewardship:

> Stewardship typically has been turned into a yearly campaign for funds and an attempt to get people to devote their service to the church by teaching in the church school, singing in the choir, being on the vestry, or assisting in the liturgy. A yearly pledge of time, talent and money, based upon programmatic budgetary needs to run an institution, is a strange understanding of stewardship.

In place of this "strange understanding," Westerhoff offers a much fuller definition of personal stewardship. He says:

> Stewardship is nothing less than a complete life style, a total accountability and responsibility before God. Stewardship is what we do after we say we believe, that is, after we give our love, loyalty and trust to God, from whom each and every aspect of our lives comes as a gift. As members of God's household, we are subject to God's economy or stewardship, that is, God's plan to reconcile the whole world and bring creation to its proper end. (Westerhoff, 1983.)

But if stewardship is "nothing less than a complete life style," what does the concept of stewardship add to our understanding of Christian life? Indeed, what does it mean to be a good steward, and why is it important for individual Christians and Christian institutions to practice the virtue of stewardship?

As described by Ronald E. Vallet in *The Stepping Stones of the Steward*, the importance of stewardship lies in the conviction that everything a Christian says or does is offered on behalf of another:

> In the Bible the steward is depicted as a person who is given the responsibility of managing something belonging to someone else. The steward is thus responsible to the owner. At the same time, the steward is not simply a passive caretaker of what has been entrusted to him or her. (Vallet, 1989.)

Because the steward is a full representative of the owner, he or she is empowered to make decisions and to take action on matters of importance—always conscious that the steward will have to render an account for his or her actions. Thus, the good steward is not hesitant, indecisive, or unable to act but is fully able to stand in the place of the master and represent his or her interests.

The aspect of Christian stewardship that calls for more than "passive caretaking" is of central importance to the new (or renewed) understanding of stewardship that is necessary if theological schools are to meet the challenges of the twenty-first century. Indeed, it can be argued that there has also been a devaluation of the concept of institutional stewardship that has reduced it to a passive, caretaking function. As a result, seminary leaders have not been sufficiently challenged to take risks or to be creative in the development of their school's resources, but have been content to rely on traditional sources of funding that do not threaten the status quo.

As the APPA/Lilly study makes clear, simply "taking care of" seminary facilities is no longer good enough. What's needed now at each theological school is a decisive plan of action that can fully develop its physical resources and make them an integral part of the school's overall mission.

This kind of decisive action represents a more active approach to the stewardship of seminary facilities. It also demands that the needs of the physical plant be considered in light of the academic and pastoral objectives of the seminary through a program of careful, mission-oriented planning.

As good stewards, seminary leaders are challenged to do the kind of integrated planning that can interrelate the needs of academic programs (and other facets of life in a contemporary theological school) with the human, physical, and financial resources of the institution. Because theological schools do not have unlimited resources, priorities have to be established and decisions need to be made about what is most important (or most urgent). Because these decisions should never be made in a vacuum, integrated planning provides seminary leaders with a context for making choices about matters of conflicting value and/ or urgency.

This is good stewardship, but it is also good planning. In fact, as many theological schools have discovered during the past two decades, not all forms of planning are successful, or even helpful. Good planning should be simple, value-oriented, and fully integrated into the school's decision-making processes. It should also facilitate (and not obstruct) the mission of theological education and the development of the resources that are needed to carry out this mission.

Eugene Hensell, president-rector of St. Meinrad School of Theology, talked about planning to participants in the APPA/Lilly workshops on seminary facilities in May 1991. He noted that planning efforts have been known to fail, and when they do, it is usually for one or more of the following reasons:

- Lack of trust resulting in fundamental disagreements about the mission or direction of an institution.

- Disagreements over the legitimacy and effectiveness of planning, which is perceived as merely a "waste of time."
- Planning processes or structures that are separated from decision-making processes or structures.
- Unwillingness to face unpleasant issues or tough choices.
- Inaccurate information, analyses, or assumptions.
- Processes that have become overly rigid and inflexible.
- Inability to deal with the uncertainty of future events or the need to be ready for what is unexpected or unwelcome.
- Unrealistic expectations about what planning is or what it can accomplish. (Hensell, 1991.)

The experiences that many schools of theology have had with bad planning have helped to identify some of the factors that are essential for successful planning. First and foremost is the understanding that planning is a function of leadership. In fact, it is the discipline that leaders use to help them articulate a vision and to set direction for the future of a theological school. With this in mind, good planning requires the endorsement and active participation of a school's leaders—the board, administration, and faculty. It also requires a willingness to focus the lens of planning activities on issues and concerns that are of fundamental importance to the school and its future—especially if such issues are unpleasant or controversial.

In addition, Hensell identified the following characteristics of good planning:

- It provides for flexibility and regular adjustment to changing circumstances and unexpected events.
- Successes and failures can be measured.
- Planners are realistic about resources (human, physical, and financial).
- Communication channels are open and effective.
- There is regular discussion of trends and their possible implications.
- It looks outward—focusing on the school in relation to its external environment. (Hensell, 1991.)

As a means for exercising good stewardship, planning involves three major activities. First, it requires boards, administrators, and faculty to be willing to let go of old patterns of thinking and acting and to be open to new ways of leading theological schools. Second, planning challenges the seminary to look outward to the external environment, and to anticipate the impact that political, economic, and cultural changes will have on theological education. Third, good planning invites seminary leaders to affirm what is substantive and essential in their traditions, while at the same time establishing new patterns of teaching and administration to adapt theological schools to changing circumstances and emerging needs.

This kind of planning, in which the leaders of a theological school become stewards of the seminary's future, is essential if theological schools in the United States and Canada are to develop the resources they need to address their deferred maintenance needs and, at the same time, develop new sources of funding for current programs and for endowments. In this context, good stewardship must also involve good fundraising.

To deal successfully with a $1.9 million capital renewal problem, and at the same time maintain a strong annual fund and a healthy endowment, the "average" seminary needs more than an average development program. Indeed, even without this significant backlog of deferred maintenance needs, it is clear that seminaries cannot afford to rely on traditional funding sources alone if they wish to keep pace with the growing demands of every aspect of contemporary theological education. Today, the challenges are so great that they require nothing less than an outstanding development effort, including:

- Full engagement of seminary leaders in the total development process. This includes articulating the seminary's mission and goals, cultivating relationships between the seminary and its constituencies, and personal solicitation of major gifts.

- A clear and compelling case for investment, outlining all the reasons why individuals and groups should choose to invest in the mission and goals of a theological school, as well as detailed strategies for communicating this case.

- A comprehensive, integrated approach to fundraising that seeks to match the needs and interests of donors with the seminary's current and long-range objectives through a logical progression from giving to the annual fund, to gifts for capital projects, to planned gifts for endowment purposes.

This is good fundraising, but it is also good stewardship of the philanthropic resources that each seminary community has available to it—namely, those individual and collective stewards who share the values of a theological school and who, therefore, have reasons of their own for investing their time, talent, and treasure in the mission and goals of a theological school.

The APPA/Lilly study presents theological schools with much more than data about roofs, windows, boilers, and safety systems. It challenges seminary leaders to:

1. Reexamine the important role that physical facilities play in the mission and goals of a theological school.

2. Develop a new understanding of the call to Christian stewardship.

In addition, this study invites all who care about the future of theological education to become more active in developing the human, physical, and financial resources that are absolutely necessary to the growth and development of theological education.

Yes, seminary leaders have been reasonably good caretakers of their institutions' physical resources. But theological education in the 1990s and beyond requires a more active form of stewardship. To look ahead to the needs of the twenty-first century, and to plan for growth in an era of decline, requires a profound act of hope. It also requires the kind of visionary leadership that truly understands how the physical structures of the seminary campus become symbols of the presence of God and partners with us in the mission of theological education.

CHRISTA R. KLEIN

CHAPTER 6

Governance and Campus Renewal

Whatever the motivation, seminary leaders who fail to cultivate trustee participation in governance are robbing the institution of a vital resource.

How will decisions about the repair and renewal of campus facilities be made? The issues surrounding capital renewal pose challenges and opportunities to a theological school's system of governance. The very steps taken to formulate a course of action will change or reinforce patterns in the ongoing conversation between the administration and governing board.

In this report, when Dan Conway argues for institutional planning, Joe O'Neill pleads for greater denominational funding, and Walt Schaw calls for a portfolio approach to facilities assets, they are proposing perspectives to be considered by these conversation partners. This chapter will consider ways to structure the conversation itself among those who govern.

By legal right and moral responsibility, governing boards must adopt the policies for dealing with deferred maintenance. When a board adopts the annual budget, takes action on the reallocation of funds for emergency repairs, or approves a plan for campus renewal, trustees are making decisions about the housing of the institution.

How early and how deeply should they be involved in such deliberations? And should the whole board be informed and invited to discuss these matters at length, or only those trustees with the pertinent expertise? Where should the details be hammered out—between the property committee and an appropriate administrator, or in an executive committee that meets more frequently?

Corporate Responsibility

Policy development can occur in many ways. But one central principle should undergird any arrangement: the board's authority is no less than corporate. Board members or committees with expertise on buildings and grounds do not have formal authority. Only when the whole board formally adopts a proposed course of action does the particular wisdom of an individual trustee or group of trustees gain its authority.

Nevertheless, if such action is no more than the proverbial rubber stamp, the very spirit of trusteeship has been violated. Routine ratification without prior deliberation both neglects the skills and experience that board members bring to the table and deprives them of the satisfaction that comes from knowing they have contributed to the life of the school. Administrators and board officers who settle for this pattern of governance may be acting less from suspicion or cynicism about the board's role than from fear that an informed board will be a meddlesome board. Unfortunately, whatever the motivation, seminary leaders who fail to cultivate trustee participation in governance are robbing the institution of a vital resource.

For board action to be meaningful for the institution and for trustees themselves, it must be an exercise in governance, not management. Conventional wisdom states that the board governs, while the staff manages or handles daily operations. Ordinarily the distinction between the two behaviors is ambiguous; during crisis, the boundary becomes especially permeable. Nevertheless, the characteristic emphases of management and governance are clear. Management sees that things get done. Governance checks whether these doings keep the institution on course.

The province of governance is the institution as a whole and its constancy and excellence in pursuing its purposes (Chait and Taylor, 1989). The venerable Western practice of lay governance— governance by outsiders rather than insider professionals— emerged out of the conviction that institutions serving the community ought to be governed by community representatives for the sake of continuity and quality.

Boards of theological schools may have a more difficult time attending to governance than the governing boards of other larger private colleges and universities. First, because the schools lack resources, they may select board members to gain access to free expertise. In the best cases such technical knowledge will be helpful for setting the direction and evaluating the work of those hired by the institution. But more often than not, board members are themselves asked to supply the expertise as part of their contribution to the school.

While laudable and leading to great expressions of commitment, such efforts may also entail an unexpected drawback. Trustee experts may learn to limit their focal point to a single area of operations. They may lose the wider perspective necessary for the board to see things whole and ensure that the institution is faithful in its pursuit of its vocation.

A second source of difficulty derives from the way board members are selected to represent constituencies. If their primary identity is and remains as representatives, they will be more interested in monitoring particular aspects of the organization than in developing critical loyalty to the institution as a whole. They may not work for strengthening the quality of governance by the whole board, but rather for pursuing their own particular agenda. This form of trusteeship whittles away at corporate purpose and can contribute to institutional drift.

While individuals ought to bring to the board their rich personal histories—including their age, gender and ethnic identities, regional church membership, theological convictions, and work experience—their primary concern as trustees must be the school and its purposes. If they cannot develop loyalty to those aims and the corporate pursuit of them, they have abandoned their primary role in governance.

Learning To See Things Whole

A commitment to governance on the part of the board depends upon a particular kind of learning. Recent writings by Peter Senge of MIT's Sloan School of Management explore the growing conviction that in the 1990s the most successful corporations, and by extension, nonprofit organizations as well, will be "learning organizations"—those that can adapt to an accelerated rate of change. But Senge himself argues that adaptation alone is not enough. Adaptation can too easily be interpreted as merely a technique for coping or survival. Learning arises from a deeper motivation, a desire to be creative. Learning "is an impulse to be generative, to expand our capability." Generative learning can only occur when people are invited to view the systemic sources of problems and not simply the symptoms (Senge, 1990).

For example, if the backlog in deferred maintenance is viewed as no more than a list of problems to be solved by those committed employees who, despite small staff and underfunding, have thus far managed to keep up appearances in noteworthy ways, then learning will be superficial and the longer-term threats to institutional purposes cannot be addressed. Other chapters in this report have already pointed out systemic reasons for the symptom of backlog. Dan Conway views the symptom as evidence of the absence of planning; Joe O'Neill as evidence of the shrinking support for theological education in the denominations; and Walt Schaw as the absence of a conceptual investment framework. All three are pointing the way to the systemic thinking required if theological schools are to function as learning organizations in their environment.

The locus for this learning about the institution should be the board room. The chief executive, with the help of the board chairperson and administrative staff, must function as the board's teacher so that trustees gain more insightful views of current reality. Information about the state of the institution should be shaped initially to provide structural analyses that go beyond the province of any one committee and any single facilities problem.

When trustees are schooled in this manner, they are prepared not only to deal with the policy issues surrounding the maintenance and renewal of the campus, but they are also learning an approach that can shape their agenda and enable them to pursue their primary work of governance. When trustees develop a propensity for asking "why" questions, they are testifying to the value of generative learning.

Another word about learning. Trustees have few other rewards for their service than learning. Learning deepens commitment and also provides them with new perspectives on their own life's work and other voluntary service. Trustees shaped by learning for the sake of governance in a theological institution may become the leaven for renewal elsewhere in society and the church.

Policy Focus

The way boards participate in the conversation about the maintenance and renewal of facilities should depend upon the level and stage of policy development. Richard Chait and Barbara Taylor, drawing on the research of others, recommend that boards concentrate their energy on the highest levels of policy and the earliest stages of policy development (Chait and Taylor, 1989). The highest policy level involves questions of institutional direction, priorities, and principles that will guide other decisions.

Once an evaluation of campus facilities has been completed, probing ought to begin at this level. Does the shape, condition, and location of the campus enhance the institution's ability to pursue its vocation or mission? Given current social and religious trends, what are the major physical obstacles and opportunities in the pursuit of that vocation? Which priorities implicit in the mission should govern how decisions will be made about the facilities?

A wide-ranging discussion in the board of these kinds of issues requires special planning and hosting. Such a conversation cannot occur within an allotted few minutes during the regular business agenda. Nor should it occur without advance preparation of materials that will help the board see the whole picture. The chief executive may want to work with either a special task force, made up of staff and board leaders, or a standing committee of the board to design an educational event to explore the issue. The options include adding a retreat day or educational forum to a regular board meeting.

Among the materials prepared for the board should be a modified and abbreviated version of the facilities audit report. This version should be designed to invite a governance, not a management, perspective. By both naming problems and issues raised by the condition of the physical plant and projecting how these will affect the school's capacity to pursue its mission, such a document will promote discussion at the appropriate policy level. Providing the audit report itself could keep board members bogged down with concerns about management details. The goal of such a meeting would be to explore and build consensus around the policy objectives for any program to renew or replace facilities.

Once the objectives are in place, then the administration and any board standing committee has the guidance it needs to formulate particular policies. At this stage in policy development, the administration is responsible for conducting wide consultation within the institution and keeping the board alerted to policy options. Once a policy has been shaped, then the administration (and, perhaps in this case, the board's property committee) should present recommendations to the board for action in such a way that the board is fully educated. The full board should hear why the committee recommends one course of action over others and how the process of consultation led to this decision. The committee should also recommend both a procedure for following the policy and a calendar to evaluate the results. In these discussions, the board's primary charge is not to serve as a second editor, but to raise questions about the policy's adequacy to the objectives it is designed to meet.

During the implementation, the board should step back, but expect to be kept up to date by those administrators charged with executing the policy. When board members have particular expertise, they may be assigned selectively and temporarily by the chief executive and board chair for a particular role. Great care should be taken that such participation does not replace the learning required of staff members to do their jobs. The board or its executive committee may also be involved where spot checking is appropriate to ensure that the quality and direction of staff performance conforms with the policy. Finally, the board receives reports from the chief executive covering the evaluation of the results.

Conclusion

This skeletal outline of an approach to policy development demonstrates one arrangement for maintaining the board's focus on its governance role. In the wake of the process, board members should be familiar enough with the issues that they can explain their decisions to others. They should be able to answer questions about why this school at this time is undertaking this renovation or construction project, and how the effort will be funded. Informed trustees become effective advocates to the school's various publics. The care of buildings and grounds offers unique opportunities in governance. As boards learn about this aspect of institutional life, trustees have the opportunity to join with the staff in building a common understanding of the institution's history and vocation. Buildings evoke the past and shelter a school's present purposes. Their aging and decay and the ebb and flow in their use provide vivid reminders that time, as the familiar hymn says, is "like an ever rolling stream."

At the same time, through their work for institutional renewal, governing boards participate in God's ongoing creation of the world. Theology students who are privileged to attend those schools governed through learning may come away knowing about standards of institutional care and creativity that will shape their own ministries among God's people.

RON CASON

Tales From an Audit:

Church of God School of Theology

It came as a great surprise to learn that our greatest and most urgent maintenance needs existed in our two newest buildings.

CHAPTER 7

The Church of God School of Theology is located in Cleveland, Tennessee, a progressive city nestled in the foothills of the Smoky Mountains. Our seasonal climate, major transportation advantages, productive labor force, exceptional quality of life, and natural beauty all combine to make this area an ideal place to live, work, and grow. Easy accessibility to Interstate 75 allows residents to reach the metropolitan areas of Atlanta, Knoxville, and Nashville in two hours by car.

The seminary is located in the central section of Cleveland adjacent to Lee College (our undergraduate institution) and the Church of God Publishing House, and is minutes from the International Offices of the Church of God. The proximity of the seminary to these institutions affords the students employment opportunities as well as ongoing interaction with denominational leaders.

Established in 1975 as the only graduate institution of our denomination, the seminary is situated on seven acres and consists of two major buildings: the primary building, built in 1980, and the library, built in 1985. In addition, there are four support-type buildings that average forty years of age: O'Neal Center, Godin Center (two housing units), and the Office of Ministerial Care. We are currently constructing an eighteen-unit apartment complex that will be occupied in early 1992.

We arranged to conduct a thorough facilities audit, and assumed that it would reveal that our major deferred maintenance problems are associated with our older structures. It therefore came as a great surprise to learn that our greatest and most urgent maintenance needs existed in our two newest buildings.

Informing the Board

Our facilities audit was conducted by a local firm with expertise in these kind of evaluations. Work began in February 1991, and the completed audit was presented to the School of Theology Board of Directors in April 1991. At this time a presentation was given to the board by the coordinator of special projects, including a presentation of APPA's video, "The Decaying American Campus." Each member also received a summary report on the results of the facilities audit.

The board was shocked by the extent and scope of our maintenance problems and the physical deterioration of what they considered to be newer structures with relatively few needed repairs. The total funds needed to maintain our physical facilities over the next ten years amounted to $669,349; of this amount, only $43,014 represented needed repairs to our older properties. The primary building, occupied in 1991, needs $243,155 in maintenance repairs over the next ten years and the library, a structure that is only six years old, was determined to need repairs at a ten-year cost of $383,180.

The board was also shown a series of photos taken by the auditing firm that verified the severity of the problem. The question was asked all around: "How can this be? Why are our newer buildings in such desperate need of repair?" The answer concerned problems related to original design and construction.

The Primary Building

The primary building is a contemporary, two-story, white brick structure reflecting modern architectural design. It is now clear that this building is an architect's dream and a maintenance worker's nightmare. The design included curved walls that have allowed water to penetrate into stairwell areas because of runoff over the roof and down the side of these curved areas. The roof drainage system was not designed in the beginning to handle this problem. The installation of flashing to divert water away from the curved wall areas would have prevented a great deal of the damage discovered through the audit.

In addition, the building was originally constructed with downspouts inside the walls to contribute to the contemporary look of the exterior. These downspouts have been impossible to maintain, and as a result water has penetrated the interior walls. When our APPA evaluator inspected this building, he shook his head and said, "Most people try to run water out of their buildings. Your architect ran it inside." The evaluator also noted that he would not allow a building to be built with this kind of curved walls, since they are a constant source of water penetration problems.

The auditing firm had reviewed the original construction materials and costs, and had discovered that the bricks were never treated with a penetrating sealer, thus allowing even more water to invade the structure. Concurrent with this were several masonry problems, where cracks needed to be repaired and an additional expansion joint needed to be cut.

As though this were not enough, the audit further revealed that the roof needed to be replaced immediately, and there were areas of plywood decking that should also be replaced. We knew the roof was in bad shape, but discovered from the audit that it had deteriorated at a much more rapid pace as a result of improper and inadequate roof ventilation. Certain sections of the roof had not been ventilated at all, causing excessive heat build-up and quicker deterioration of the shingles in some areas. Insulation had been positioned over vent areas, and a new continuous vent had to be installed in the soffit area.

We also learned from the audit that our HVAC system had not been properly maintained. The refrigerated aftercooler on the control air system needed immediate replacement, and a single-stage air compressor needed to be replaced with a new duplex one. The air handling unit cooling coils and inlet vanes had not been cleaned in a long time, and one inlet vane operator had to be replaced as soon as possible.

The board was made aware of the fact that many of our current maintenance problems existed because original construction had not been properly supervised and thought out. It was decided that an appeal would be made to our denomination for assistance on urgent items, and then endowment funds would be solicited to handle deferred maintenance needs in the future.

The facilities audit was presented to our denominational officials by the dean of the seminary, who is responsible for maintenance, along with the chairman of the board's physical facilities and grounds committee. The denomination's reaction was much the same as the board's, and the seriousness and scope of these problems compelled them to take immediate action. Within a week after the appeal was presented to them, the denomination instructed us to gather a list of urgent needs that needed to be addressed in the next ninety days. Our facilities audit had set priorities for repairs as well as providing cost estimates, and we presented a list of urgent items totaling $49,010.

The denomination compared our list with their copy of the audit report, and discussed these needs with representatives of the auditing firm. They agreed with our assessment of those items needing immediate attention, and appropriated $50,000 for urgent repairs to be made in the next ninety days.

The Library

The library's deferred maintenance problems, involving repairs totaling $383,180 over the next ten years, are still to be addressed. A unique situation concerning the original decision to build the library resources for the Church of God School of Theology involves the role of the Pentecostal Resource Center (PRC).

The PRC is a separate entity that was created by a resolution passed at our denominational assembly in 1980. This resolution specifically states that the PRC is created to serve the "present and projected ministries of Lee College, the Church of God School of Theology, and other educational institutions of the Church of God." Hence, the programs of the PRC go beyond serving the needs of the seminary, to serve Lee College and the general church. The PRC houses the William G. Squires Library, which integrates the library collections of the two schools, and the Hal Bernard Dixon Pentecostal Research Center, which contains resources on the Pentecostal/Charismatic movement and the archives of the Church of God. Although both institutions are served by the PRC, the denomination owns the building and was instrumental in its construction.

The facilities audit revealed numerous needed repair items on this six-year-old building, again resulting from improper design and poor construction practices. For example, like the primary building, the library's bricks had not been treated with a penetrating sealer. The library also is experiencing hot and cold areas as a result of an ineffective perimeter unit heater system—the fans are not powerful enough to move air to the end of ductwork. A defective metal panel veneer system was installed on exterior walls and is taking on water at the joints and becoming damaged from moisture and freeze-thaw cycles. Replacement or repair of this system is estimated to cost $67,000.

The manufacturer has been contacted and there may be some relief through a warranty on the product. However, the system was taken off the market by the manufacturer the same year it was installed on our building.

To add insult to injury, the library was constructed on a former lake bed, and underground springs make water penetration into the elevator shaft a constant problem. Again, inadequate planning and oversight during construction has precipitated many of these problems. It will come as no surprise that the same architect was used on both the primary building and the library.

A separate appeal for $100,000 has been made to the denomination for urgent repairs on the PRC, while we explore the possibility of warranty contracts requiring contractors to return and remedy some problems. The company that installed the ductwork and blower system has agreed to make repairs to improve air flow in the building. Other contractors have been approached, as well as manufacturers of defective materials.

Conclusion

The denomination is now aware of the seriousness of deferred maintenance in our educational institutions. As a result of the APPA/Lilly project, the building that houses our denominational offices was discovered to need more than $200,000 in immediate repairs. Money has already been appropriated and repairs have begun.

The immediate benefits from participation in this project are clear. Even more exciting are future possibilities for funding as a result of this endeavor. We are thankful to Lilly Endowment, Inc. for its continued commitment to theological education, and to APPA for the expertise and training they are providing this and other institutions of higher learning.

8

Meeting the Challenge:
Midwestern Baptist Theological Seminary

Lilly's funding and APPA's expertise opened the door to a new and productive approach to facilities maintenance.

Midwestern Baptist Theological Seminary is a graduate professional school committed to the education of persons preparing for Christian ministry. The seminary is owned and operated by the Southern Baptist Convention of churches by which it was established in 1957.

The seminary's 200-acre campus is located at the heart of Kansas City North. The site, immediately adjacent to Interstate Highway 29, is fifteen minutes from downtown Kansas City and the international airport. It also has convenient access to three interstate highways, as well as to numerous shopping centers.

The campus is located on the historic Vivion Farms estate, a landmark in the region since the late nineteenth century. The campus expanse includes broad rolling meadows and beautiful woodlands with much virgin timber, including several giant oak trees that are more than 300 years old.

The main academic campus facilities and the residential complex occupy no more than one-fourth of the total campus acreage, which serves to highlight the spatial beauty of the campus setting. The majority of the campus facilities are situated on a hilltop giving the seminary high visibility in the surrounding community.

Facilities Overview

The initial building program in 1958-59 provided basic administrative and academic facilities. The administration center, library, and auditorium are clustered around an open courtyard featuring a fifty-foot spire that is represented in the school's logo. Classroom facilities and faculty offices are situated on the other side of the primary campus drive.

The architecture selected for these first facilities features a contemporary design utilizing extensive covered walkways and courtyards connecting the various buildings. Materials selected for building exteriors were gray Texas fieldstone, and blue Mediterranean decorative tile, combined with large expanses of single-glazed exterior window panels.

During the 1960s, additional classroom facilities, a new residence hall for single students, and the first complex of married-student housing were added. The 1970s brought additional student housing, as well as faculty offices and renovation of the first classroom building.

The 1980s saw the construction of a child development center, plus additional housing for married-student families, bringing the total number of family housing units on campus to 143. These facilities include 60,000 square feet for general academic and administrative use, and 165,000 square feet for student family housing. The campus complex supports a student body averaging approximately 600 students in annual cumulative enrollment.

The Problem

The capital funding provided by the sponsoring denomination for the initial academic facilities was limited. The trustees and administration worked hard to stretch available funds sufficiently to provide the necessary buildings and equipment for the newly established institution. Much attention was given to the aesthetics and functional convenience of the original buildings, perhaps at the expense of some of the structural, mechanical, and electrical infrastructures.

The young seminary also experienced serious financial adversity during the first ten years of its life due to circumstances beyond its control. The combination of these factors resulted in serious deferral of both routine and preventive maintenance. By the mid-1970s, maintenance and equipment deficiencies had developed into serious structural and systems problems.

The Struggle

Structural and maintenance problems were addressed beginning in 1975 with the initiation of building exterior restoration and complete renovation of specific facilities, including faculty offices, classrooms, and the residence hall. Concerted attention was given to the mechanical and electrical systems and a program of routine maintenance, and some minimal preventive maintenance was initiated. During the 1980s, increased attention was given to such items as roof maintenance, water and gas line replacement, basic equipment upgrading, and general regulatory compliance issues.

Significant progress in both regular and preventive maintenance was made during the years between 1975 and 1990.

The nature of that activity, however, focused almost exclusively on dealing with crises and challenges due to the original design limitation and/or the early years of deferred maintenance.

The Opportunity

The support provided by the Lilly Endowment, in conjunction with a program of evaluation prepared by APPA, enabled Midwestern Seminary to take a giant step forward in confronting the deferred maintenance challenges inherent in its campus facilities. Lilly's funding and APPA's expertise opened the door to a new and productive approach to facilities maintenance.

The workshops provided by APPA were attended by the seminary president, the vice president for business affairs, and the director of campus operations. These resources, along with materials provided and individual consultations, helped prepare the seminary administration to approach the matter of facilities maintenance on a holistic and realistic long-range basis.

The initial report prepared by our APPA evaluator served as a basis for seminary staff actions in setting parameters and outlining requirements for the comprehensive facilities audit. This audit was completed in the spring of 1991. The team of architects and engineers detailed more than $3.5 million in deferred maintenance needs among the seminary's academic facilities and student housing units.

The review focused on four areas: architectural, structural, mechanical, and electrical components of the facilities. It revealed substantial behind-the-scenes deterioration of facilities subsystems. Many of these challenges are immediate and urgent. Indeed, 73 percent of all deferred maintenance chronicled in the audit is recommended to be dealt with during the first three years of the projected ten-year renewal cycle ($2,678,346 of the total projection of $3,672,692).

The Benefits

The facilities audit now functions as an indispensable tool in the seminary's planning process and financial projections. It provides extensive detail regarding deferred maintenance needs, and enables the seminary administration and trustees to establish realistic priorities as they address these needs in the context of total program projections and budget resources.

The facilities audit has benefited the seminary in an immediate and dramatic way as well. During the initial phases of the evaluation process, serious deterioration was discovered in the structural steel supporting the second-level balconies of the multipurpose seminary classroom/student center building. These structures consisted of five-inch steel posts inside stone columns. The steel posts at several points were seriously rusted to the point of being structurally deficient, thus endangering the integrity of the weight-bearing columns.

This condition was addressed immediately during the spring and summer of 1991, and the posts were replaced by more adequate steel columns. The structural integrity of this building was recovered as a direct result of the facilities audit project. This represents considerable savings over what might have been required had the deficiency not been discovered in a timely manner.

Midwestern Seminary was able to complete its extensive facilities audit and all related projects at an expenditure of approximately $34,000. The seminary requested and received assistance to establish a computerized maintenance/work order system for the entire campus, and to provide a program of continuing advance professional training for the campus operations staff.

The Challenge

A summary of the facilities audit was presented to the building and grounds committee of the seminary trustees in October 1991, and through that committee was reported to the entire board of trustees. The results of the audit also are being incorporated into the institutional self-study currently being conducted as a part of the seminary's ten-year accreditation evaluation program.

The audit detail and financial projections are also helpful as the seminary administration and trustees engage in a comprehensive study regarding long-range land use and endowment development of the 200-acre campus properties.

The Lilly Endowment grant, in conjunction with the resources provided by APPA, has enabled Midwestern Seminary to establish a comprehensive, intensive, and detailed analysis of deferred maintenance needs, plus a projected schedule for addressing those needs during the next ten years. This project would never have been accomplished without the resources and encouragement provided by the APPA/Lilly project.

The challenge involved in meeting deferred maintenance needs is formidable, but it is now feasible and manageable because it is a known quantity with which the seminary can deal in its financial planning and annual budget commitments.

JERRY L. SCHMALENBERGER

A Committee Approach:
Pacific Lutheran Theological Seminary

In order for the campus to survive, administrators had simply ignored maintenance during its entire forty-one-year history.

When I arrived at Pacific Lutheran Theological Seminary in August 1988, everything leaked. Not only that, I found antiquated and nearly unusable boilers; wood trim on most of the buildings that was bare and quickly deteriorating; overloaded and shorted-out electrical circuits, HVAC controls frozen in a particular position; trapped groundwater that was causing settlement of two buildings; old gas lines that had so deteriorated that one could smell the strong odor of natural gas near several buildings; and eight and a half acres of seminary campus so overgrown with California vegetation that it was out of control.

The seminary began operations in 1950 when several supporting synods of the Lutheran Church purchased two properties on the top of one of the highest hills in Berkeley near eight other seminaries and the University of California's Berkeley campus. The hilltop campus has added to the two Spanish mansions a dorm for single people, a brick library building, and a chapel. Forty-two apartment units were purchased in downtown Berkeley.

Since its beginning, the seminary has never had adequate funding. In order for the campus to survive, administrators had simply ignored maintenance during its entire forty-one-year history.

Then came the earthquake of 1989. The dormitory roof was pulled apart at the seams, the corner of one building sank further from the structure, and the board of directors became painfully aware of the need to assess the safety of facilities in earthquake-prone California.

I advertised in nearby Lutheran congregations for volunteers to serve on a property committee. These people would be the stewards of the facilities now owned by the seminary. Monthly

Saturday-morning meetings began with this group of highly professional leaders, including an engineer, a geologist, the head of maintenance for a large chain of banks, a retired maintenance person, a contractor, and a carpenter.

The committee used its Lilly Endowment grant and APPA's expertise to inspect the campus, which produced a long list of physical needs for every one of the seminary's buildings. The grant also made possible an energy audit by a professional firm and a seismic study by a local engineering firm that specialized in earthquake damage and retrofitting of buildings.

The property committee then took all these reports and information and ranked them by priority on a computer. There is now a plan of action to move the seminary from crisis maintenance to a complete program of preventive maintenance.

At the same time that the property committee was meeting with the president, he also formed a development committee. This committee considered the physical needs as well as all the other financial needs of the institution, and was headed by a member of the board, who reported the committee's progress periodically to the full board. Under the leadership of the vice president for seminary advancement, a major gifts campaign was outlined. The campaign set a goal of $7 million over a three-year period, and included $900,000 for immediate maintenance needs and a $1 million endowment that will produce funds annually to keep the seminary in first-class operating condition.

At an academic convocation on Founder's Day, I was able to announce that after one year of visiting major donors and conducting a feasibility study, $3 million of the $7 million goal had either been received, was promised, or will be received within the three-year campaign period. The second phase of the property committee's work is to select contractors to perform the identified facilities work over the next couple of years as income is realized from the campaign.

Replacing the two old and "holey" gas lines is anticipated to cut our utilities bill by one-third. In addition, as a result of the energy study conducted by the property committee, we have received a grant of $7,000, and a loan of $7,000 has been received from the State of California. The committee is presently overseeing the installation of more energy-efficient electrical appliances.

When the board meets twice each year, the chair of the property committee provides advice to the board's resource committee, which allocates money for the seminary's work. The seminary advancement committee through its chair, who is also a member of the board, continues to update the board on the success of the major gifts campaign for the funds to carry out the work.

Soon there will be no more leaky roofs, already the smell of gas has been eliminated, the wood is being restored, new electrical appliances will be installed soon, seismic retrofitting will be completed by summer 1992, and campus landscaping is being performed as I write this.

APPA and Lilly have brought a keen sense of stewardship to the Lutherans on the west coast who take much pride in their theological seminary.

MAUREEN SEPKOSKI

CHAPTER

10

Creative Financing:
Catholic Theological Union

Operating reserves were needed to support the education budget while new programming and recruitment efforts got under way. Thus, funds for capital improvements had to come from elsewhere.

In 1988-89, Catholic Theological Union at Chicago (CTU), one of the largest Roman Catholic graduate schools of theology in the country, found itself facing a dilemma shared by many other theological schools. Shifting enrollment patterns had placed pressure on the school's facilities and capacity to offer programming and housing to a changing student body. The thirty religious communities who send students to CTU for their Master of Divinity degrees had a decreasing number of these students.

At the same time there was substantial growth in populations of more nontraditional students who wished to prepare for ministerial work at the master's level or who wished to pursue continuing education. However, these students needed access to evening and weekend programming as well as affordable, secure housing. For the sake of its mission and its own survival, the school had to respond to these changing circumstances.

CTU is located in an older urban neighborhood along the lake front in Chicago, close to four other theological schools and the University of Chicago. Our campus has three buildings. The main building is a ten-story former residential hotel with living space on the upper floors, a library and faculty and administrative offices on the middle floors, and a food service and common area on the first floor. Another five-story building contains sixty-four efficiency apartments. The third building was acquired in 1985, but was not converted to the school's use until 1988-89. It contains one-bedroom and efficiency apartments. In 1988-89, the school rented its classroom space during weekdays from the neighboring Sinai Temple School.

CTU's board adopted a building plan in 1988 that addressed the need for new and changed facilities. The first element was the need for additional classroom and assembly space that would be available in the evenings, on weekends, and for summer programs. Courtyard space attached to the main building was available for a classroom annex.

A second element was the recognition that housing operations were a strategic as well as financially important factor for the school, but that substantial renovation and repairs were necessary before the residential buildings could be fully occupied.

However, the school had a relatively small endowment. Its operating reserves were needed to support the education budget while new programming and recruitment efforts got under way. Thus, funds for capital improvements had to come from elsewhere. As a result, the administration and board developed a program of long-term, interest-free loans with the religious communities who sent students to the school and who had a high stake in its continued health.

An overall goal of approximately $1.2 million was set, and the amount to be requested of each community was determined by prorating the overall amount according to the size of the membership of each group. Each community was asked to offer the school a loan to be paid in over a five-year period, and to be paid back by the school at no interest over a fifteen-year period. The plan obviously was to give the school the use of the money up front to take care of needed projects and through the accrued interest to also ensure the school's capacity to pay back the loans to the community.

The administration approached each of the communities personally, and gave them a full briefing on the school's financial position and what projects the borrowed funds would support. At the same time, the school was inaugurating its own development program so that the administration could assure the communities that the institution would do its part to secure funding from other sources as well.

The response from the communities was excellent, with all but two of the thirty joining the loan program. The program was launched in the spring of 1988, with payments beginning the next fiscal year. Careful financial management and monitoring of the program by the administration and the board has made sure that the school retains the capacity to repay the loans, even though several of the communities—not unexpectedly—have indicated that they may forgive all or part of the loans when the payback period begins.

Although a loan program rather than a direct grant, this approach had the advantage of making the capital drive more acceptable to religious communities that were already offering considerable support to the school. At the same time, having such a drive enabled the school to have needed capital in hand for some of its immediate needs, and provided the communities an opportunity to renew their allegiance to the school. It also offered the president and the financial officer the chance to personally contact each key constituent, to brief them on the status and future plans of the school, and to hear their concerns and expectations. In every instance, it proved more advantageous to visit the community representatives at their own locations rather than asking them to visit the school itself.

As a result of the success of the program, a $400,000 renovation project on the third building began in the summer of 1988, and the building was fully occupied by the following spring. A new classroom annex of approximately 3,600 square feet and renovations to lounge and meeting areas in the main building were under way by the following summer. All told, $900,000 of the loan funds were used for immediate projects. The remainder is serving as an invested pool for underwriting the payback of the loans.

At the same time, the school's reserves remained available for current operations. By the end of the 1991 fiscal year, net housing operations had grown from $50,000 in the mid-1980s to $150,000. This growth, in turn, has created a new source of reserves to apply to deferred maintenance for all of our buildings. The growth in the student body also is directly tied to the availability of housing.

While this loan program was tailored to the union-model corporate structure of CTU, it could be attractive to other kinds of schools and ecclesial bodies. The same kind of allocation plan could be used by schools with their supporting congregations. One feature of CTU's plan was the determination of the monetary value of the foregone interest, and the application of this amount to the price of corporate membership for those religious communities who wished to become full corporate members of the school. Through this method the number of corporate members doubled from nine to eighteen in three years. It may be possible to adapt the foregone interest calculation to benefit donors who are not tax-exempt themselves.

FLOYD SIMMONS

CHAPTER 11

Establishing Maintenance Endowments:

Covenant Theological Seminary

Focusing on the physical plant is not a distraction from our primary purpose; it is the environment in which the educational program can thrive and develop unhampered.

Covenant Theological Seminary is an example of a small educational institution that successfully confronted the problem of an aging physical plant through a fundraising campaign for campus apartments. The program uniquely combined fundraising for these revenue-generating facilities with an endowment for the deferred maintenance of those same structures.

Many of the features of Covenant's situation are unique and favorable, yet there remain many dimensions to our story that will benefit other institutions.

Background

Covenant Theological Seminary's enrollment has nearly tripled in three years. We now have approximately 410 students, most of whom are training to be pastors.

Although Covenant enjoys being the denominational seminary of one of the most rapidly growing denominations in the United States, the Presbyterian Church in America (PCA), Covenant has trained pastors and Christian workers for dozens of denominations throughout the United States and around the world.

Covenant Theological Seminary was founded in 1956 as the seminary of a small denomination, the Reformed Presbyterian Church (Evangelical Synod). At that time the seminary shared facilities with the denomination's liberal arts school, Covenant College.

In 1964 Covenant College established its own campus in Lookout Mountain, Georgia, leaving the seminary as the sole possessor of the campus in the St. Louis suburb, Creve Coeur.

Although the denominational sponsor of the seminary had remained small, in 1982 that denomination joined the larger, and rapidly growing, Presbyterian Church in America. Formed in 1973, the PCA relied on various independent seminaries for ministerial training. However, in joining the PCA, Covenant Theological Seminary assumed the status of being the national seminary of that denomination. The denomination still maintains an active relationship with these other schools, drawing ministers from their ranks as well as Covenant's.

Deciding To Build

Even before joining PCA, members of the seminary community had hoped that Covenant would grow in enrollment and influence. The improvement of the facilities, especially housing for students, was perceived by many as an important component to change. Now, joining with the PCA provided encouragement to move forward with plans that had long been in their prayers.

A plan was proposed to the board of trustees in 1983 to build on-campus apartments. The board rejected that plan, citing the poorly maintained condition of existing campus facilities. Facility maintenance thus became a matter of high priority.

Early in 1985 a new seminary president was appointed. His mission included improving physical plant maintenance, rebuilding a facility that had either reached or was near retirement age, and addressing the then-serious issue of declining enrollment. I was hired in 1985 to assist in matters related to business and finance, but with a view toward how the physical plant could be turned around. I came to Covenant Seminary having previously served for eight years as a college physical plant director during a period of major renovations.

When I was brought on as business administrator, the seminary leadership still tended to think in terms of off-campus housing, even purchasing land on which to construct an apartment complex. However, in early 1987 an admissions consultant contracted by the seminary recommended that on-campus housing be built. It seems that some prospective students visiting the campus were deterred by the prospect of living in the less-costly neighborhoods some distance from campus. (The area surrounding Covenant Seminary is affluent, and consists primarily of single family residences.)

By this time, the performance of the physical plant department was improving, and the trustees and seminary staff were confident that new facilities could be properly maintained. In the fall of 1987, the trustees gave their approval to construct student apartments on campus.

One of the attractions to building campus apartments was their potential as a new source for funding the seminary as a whole. By raising the money through outright gifts to the seminary to construct facilities that would produce revenue, all of the revenue produced could be used to fund annual operations and set aside reserves for future repairs (deferred maintenance). Also, net funds would likely be available for support of the academic program. Handled in this manner, revenue-producing facilities would become a form of operating endowment.

Our development department took this one step further: fully funding the construction of the apartments would produce even more revenue for our mission if the seminary management, maintenance, and operation of the apartments were endowed.

This approach seemed to run counter to the conventional wisdom, which said that such an approach asked too much of donors. However, we wanted to indicate to donors that this route was in fact the best way to make the new apartments work in behalf of our core purpose as a seminary. Not only would the housing be provided, it would be cared for perpetually, and net revenue would flow permanently in support of the seminary's purpose: training people for ministry.

We determined the cost of endowing the project based on the assumption that we would need 50 percent of the amount spent for construction. This seemed to be enough to generate the necessary income for proper care of the facility.

Funding the Apartments

Our vice president for development first gained the support of two major individual donors for the concept of endowing campus housing. Then, he and the seminary president met with a foundation that had funded construction for two other buildings, the J. Oliver Buswell Jr. Library and the Robert G. Rayburn Chapel. They discovered that the foundation had been concerned about problems with the maintenance of the buildings funded in the past (apparently the foundation had kept informed about these things). But the foundation now expressed pleasure at the correction of this problem in recent years; it wanted to be sure that any facilities associated with its name were well cared for.

After the successful meeting with the foundation, the vice president for development met with an important group of donors. He was concerned that they might balk at supporting a revenue-producing and endowed program. Instead he found that the donors were excited about the concept. They could see that many ongoing benefits would flow from this one-time gift.

Participation in Planning

After the decision of the board of trustees, an architect was hired later in 1987 who worked closely with the business office, physical plant, and student services (who had helped new students locate housing). Floor plans of where students lived at the time were used to help determine needs.

The architect also developed a questionnaire that drew students, spouses, and others involved with our Family Nurture Program into the process. The responses were then reviewed by students, particularly the student council.

Since the average age of our students in 1987 was 32, and most were married with children, we focused on floor plans for two- and three-bedroom apartments. Three-bedroom apartments, much in demand by students who previously had owned their own homes, were particularly expensive and hard to find in the St. Louis area.

We decided to set rents at the market level in the neighborhoods in which students currently lived plus estimated transportation costs. Lower rents would have reduced the benefits of rent revenue for the seminary community, as well as tending to draw students out of neighborhoods with greater opportunities for church work. The involvement of our students in the ministries of local churches is integral to Covenant Seminary's objective of developing genuine pastoral skills and experience as part of the educational process.

While we wanted to provide an attractive community environment for families, these apartments also were envisioned as acceptable to younger, single students should the trends ever shift. While the national trend has not as yet changed, it is interesting to note that in 1991 we attracted a larger number of younger students. The average age of our student body, which had gone up to 35, has actually decreased back to the 1987 level of 32. The apartment complex, with its family atmosphere, seems to be attractive to a broad range of Covenant students. Single people enjoy sharing the facilities with families.

Moving In

By the fall of 1990 three buildings were fully occupied, including one building of twelve two-bedroom units and two of our six-unit, three-bedroom apartment buildings. The remaining four buildings, each containing three-bedroom units, were completed and fully occupied by summer 1991. Since construction of the project began, enrollment has soared, and the apartments were one element of many that contributed to this rapid growth.

In the fall of 1991, the last twenty-four three-bedroom apartments were ready. The apartment community on campus has created a warm environment that enhances the development of friendships and attracts new student families.

Looking Forward

We now have the means to perpetually care for the apartments, but other buildings on campus are aging and the annual operating budget is straining to keep up with rapidly increasing enrollments. In addressing this need, we began asking ourselves how we could raise funds for these repairs.

At the very time that this matter appeared on our agenda, we found that Covenant had been included among a group of seminaries chosen by the Lilly Endowment for a study of facilities. An APPA workshop already scheduled but not sponsored by Lilly presented an approach to conducting a facilities condition inspection. APPA helped us prepare a request-for-proposal to get bids for a facilities audit.

The firm we selected finished the facilities audit by spring 1991. It produced a building-by-building list of projects in order of priority over ten years. The information is on a computerized data base so that it can be updated. This is not a static report; it is a dynamic system. Information is in a format that provides various levels of detail and summary so it can be used at the simplest level to assign work, or at the highest level to inform trustees and motivate prospective donors.

We have already used the report to approach donors regarding funding. They are quite impressed that the information is so thorough. It enhances their confidence that we have a handle on the problem.

Being a small campus, our funding needs for deferred maintenance of about $2.5 million is for us a large sum. Yet we believe it is an attainable sum, particularly because it is so well defined. Of the amount needed, we had already raised about $450,000 to keep our apartments in good repair over the next ten years because their operation has been endowed.

Based on the current value of our campus facilities, we determined that an endowment of $3.6 million would provide the $180,000 (5 percent earnings use) needed for an annual maintenance and repair provision equal annually to more than 2 percent of the value of our facilities. Included in this amount is a provision for care of the grounds and improvements such as walks, roads, and campus lighting. Of this amount we had already raised $1.2 million of the endowment for the apartments.

Thus, $2.4 million would provide an endowment for the perpetual care of our campus facilities. Again, this seems to be a realistic amount to raise. As long as the operating endowment is raised with each new facility in the future, the total campus can continue to be maintained with no deferred maintenance.

This work can be done with no drain on the annual operating budget. Some may say that raising this kind of money is not feasible, but we have already experienced great enthusiasm for this type of funding. Donors can see the long-range, positive impact and the fact that such investments tie in to the overall mission for which we exist.

Future annual funding efforts can now be concentrated on the seminary's central educational programs. Focusing on the physical plant is not a distraction from our primary purpose; it is the environment in which the educational program can thrive and develop unhampered. We have found that donors can become quite excited about these concepts, as long as the case is presented properly.

WALTER A. SCHAW

CHAPTER 12

Epilogue:
Social Significance of the Project

"America is a country of such freedoms that it is possible to hold it together only through the internal discipline of Americans' fervent belief in religion."
Alexis de Tocqueville, 1835

This dictum by one of the most enduring observers of America has a special relevance as we review the physical condition of theological schools in the United States and Canada. If Tocqueville's statement holds true today, what is the condition of America and where is it heading?

Author Thomas Wolfe, in a recent speech to association executives, made an interesting prediction: "As has happened in other cultures and other centuries, an America which has been adrift for thirty years is now poised for a return to basic values as we live through the 1990s." The catalyst, Wolfe believes, will be "the end of an unprecedented expansion during which we forgot that the debts of such expansion must one day be repaid."

Who will lead this renewal into the next century? Where will these leaders come from? At the core of any answer is America's 202 theological education institutions, preparing some 56,000 students as our next generation of spiritual leaders.

This report includes a general assessment of facilities conditions at schools of theology. I suggest that those conditions have a direct bearing on our collective future.

Readily observable and measurable campus conditions give evidence of challenges and issues beyond themselves. Some reflect a struggle with survival, as once grand edifices house a fraction of their former enrollment. Others reflect chronically underfunded operations. (There is a practical limit on tuition when students have a salary expectation of only $18,000 per year.) Still other schools face major expenditures in adapting buildings to accommodate a demographic shift to older, married students.

During this study, a close relationship has developed between APPA and theological schools and their presidents. In becoming acquainted with these institutions and the people who run them, several factors stood out. One was the high level of staff dedication, from business officers struggling with extremely limited means to custodians covering far more space than reflected in national averages. We observed a tremendous belief in the value of their work by staff at schools of theology.

The other factor is a somewhat more subjective observation. There is, in our opinion, a consistent demonstration of personal leadership by the presidents of these schools. Their articulated sense of mission is greater than we have found in higher education as a whole. And I submit that, of all the essential ingredients for the future well-being of theological education in America, a sense of mission and effective leadership are truly indispensable.

"Better the end of a matter than its beginning, better patience than pride."
(Ecclesiastes 7:8,9)

Appendix A:
Technical Notes

The data presented in Chapter 1 of this report represents the responses from sixty-seven schools of theology who participated in the study, or 33.2 percent of the universe of 202 such institutions in the United States and Canada listed by the Association of Theological Schools in 1988. The research population includes forty-one schools who have been the subject of a year-long APPA/Lilly Endowment project to assess facilities conditions. In expanding the representative population for this research, a random sixty schools of theology were added.

A survey instrument, presented at the end of this Appendix, was issued to both the original and additional groups. All of the forty-one original participants responded, and twenty-five of the additional group returned verifiable data. In the former group, two-thirds of the respondents used formal facilities audits for their data, while one-third of the latter group reported from such audits. Those who did not use audits derived their data from institutional staff. In all cases, where analysis of responses gave rise to questions, the data was validated by APPA staff through telephone inquiry.

Missing values were not imputed. Averages were calculated on available responses from the institutions able to answer. In no instance, however, was more than .0635 of the total population missing from calculations. Not included in the sixty-seven respondents tabulated was a small number of surveys that were returned largely incomplete and could not be validated.

This report presents both an arithmetic mean (the average of all respondents) as well as a median (with half the respondents ranked above and half below the number presented).

The average gross institutional expenditure per student of $15,000 is known data obtained from the Association of Theological Schools. This figure was compared to data derived from respondents to the APPA/Lilly survey. The survey report of $16,020 deviates by .068 as an indicator of data reliability.

The arithmetic mean deviation can be in error if the survey results are not normally distributed. No attempt was made to distribute the sample results according to rank by student enrollment (FTE) as precisely representative of theological schools. Measurement error, however, was reduced as far as was practical.

In presenting the data in Chapter 1 as quantitative research, the possibility of error induced by the "halo" or "Hawthorne" effect has been considered, particularly with the original test group of forty-one schools. No evidence of bias was suggested by analysis, as two-thirds of these schools could support their data by formal facilities condition audits.

Throughout this report, analysis has sought to express the data in straightforward and readily understandable terms while maintaining balance and fairness in its presentation. The purpose is to present comparative findings framed as information for policy and planning at every institution. Decision rules, such as the standards for space, are presented both to focus the attention of decision makers on significant issues and to offer a framework for individual interpretation.

Sources for the research methodology applied here include *Practical Evaluation* by Dr. Michael Quinn Patton of the University of Minnesota, who also served as a reviewer for Chapters 1 through 3. The research design, development, and interpretation drew substantially from the extensive experience of APPA with the issues of deferred maintenance and capital renewal. An earlier report, *The Decaying American Campus: A Ticking Time Bomb* is cited often in this study, and represents a landmark study of this issue for all of higher education.

SEMINARY
FACILITIES FOLLOW-UP QUESTIONNAIRE

Seminary Name: _____

Address: _____

_____

Survey Completed By: _____ Phone: _____

I.   Please rank the below listed areas considered to be of
primary concern at your institution. (No. 1 being highest
priority and most important; 5 being of lowest priority or
least important):

    _____   Primary Structure: Includes items such as
foundations, building exteriors, floor and roof
systems.

    _____   Secondary Structure: Includes ceilings, walls,
windows, and doors.

    _____   Service Systems: Includes heating, cooling,
plumbing, electrical and conveying systems.

    _____   Safety Standards: Includes all areas of life,
health and safety standards.

    _____   Functional Standards: Includes adaptability,
suitability, and usage of current space.

II. Total Building Area Square Footage: _____

III. Total Amount of Deferred Maintenance_____

IV. How were totals (square footage and deferred maintenance)
obtained?

    _____   Institutional/Physical Plant Staff

    _____   Facilities Audit

    _____   Other

V.   Square Footage and Deferred Maintenance by Functional Area:

	Square Footage	$ Deferred Maintenance
A. Classroom (Classrooms/Learning Laboratories)		
B. Office (Faculty/Staff)		
C. Library (Stacks/Reading)		
D. Housing (Student/Faculty)		
E. Common Areas (Hallways/Dining/ Lounges)		
F. Service (Physical Plant/ Storage)		
G. Auxiliary (Please list type of space.)		
H. Acres Maintained (Lawns Parking Lots; Athletic & Recreation)		

VI. Total Institutional Budget Expenditures
     FY 1990-91:   _____

VII. Facilities/Physical Plant Expenditures 1990-91:

Expenditure Account	Supplies/ Equipment	Salaries	*Number Staff/Labor Type
Administration			
Architecture/Engineering			
Utilities (Non-Fuel)			
Fuel			
Maintenance/Operations			
Repairs/Renovations			
Other Services: (Please list)			
			.
Totals			

* Please code as to number of personnel and type of labor. (Example: Maintenance/Operations/3 ft. - 4 pt./A-B)
          A = Full Time/Part Time Staff
          B = Student/Work Study
          C = Contract Labor

Note: For your information, a copy of the APPA/NACUBO Classification of Accounts is attached.

VIII. Funding Plans for Deferred Maintenance (provide actual
      and/or budgeted amounts):

      FY 1990-91 _____

      FY 1991-92 _____

      FY 1992-93 _____

Appendix B:
Participating Institutions and APPA Evaluators

Institution	Evaluator
American Baptist Seminary of the West	Paul Tabolt University of California/Berkeley
Ashland Theological Seminary	Clinton Hofstetter College of Wooster
Associated Mennonite Biblical Seminaries	Don Dedrick University of Notre Dame
Athenaeum of Ohio	James Landers Xavier University
Atlantic School of Theology	William Lord, J.G. Sykes, and P.F. Howitt Dalhousie University
Austin Presbyterian Theological Seminary	H.C. Lott Jr. University of Texas/Austin
Canadian Theological Seminary	Duncan Watt University of Regina
Catholic Theological Union	Robert Getz University of Illinois/Chicago
Chicago Theological Seminary	George Preston Art Institute of Chicago
Christian Theological Seminary	Michael Gardner Butler University

Institution	Evaluator
Church of God School of Theology	Henry L. Shelby Tennessee Technological University
Claremont School of Theology	Dale M. Klein Claremont Colleges
Covenant Theological Seminary	Patrick J. Apel Maryville College/St. Louis
Dominican School of Philosophy and Theology	Mohammad Qayoumi San Jose State University
The Eastern Baptist Theological Seminary	Jack L. Knee and Bruce Rohrbach Penn State University
Eden Theological Seminary	T. Dan McCrary Washington University
Episcopal Divinity School	Leo Dunn Harvard University
Evangelical Seminary of Puerto Rico	Cristobal Santiago Turabo University
General Theological Seminary	Walter Murray and Leonard Pisano New York University
Gordon-Conwell Theological Seminary	Win Wassenar and John Holden Williams College
Hebrew Union College	Lyman Brenneman Miami University, and Richard Neidhard Member Emeritus
Iliff School of Theology	Kathy Messimer University of Colorado
Interdenominational Theological Center	James Priest Georgia Institute of Technology
Memphis Theological Seminary	Brian Foshee Rhodes College

Institution	Evaluator
Methodist Theological School in Ohio	John Tombarge Ohio Wesleyan University
Midwestern Baptist Theological Seminary	Ken Gillespie Metropolitan Community Colleges
Nazarene Theological Seminary	Donald Hatch University of Missouri/ Kansas City
New Brunswick Theological Seminary	Earl Smith and Vernie Coston Rutgers University
Oblate School of Theology	Charles Jenkins Saint Mary's University
Pacific Lutheran Theological Seminary	Arthur Sykes Peralta Community College District
Reformed Theological Seminary	Sam Polk Sr. Jackson State University
Saint Meinrad Seminary	Gary Kent Indiana University/ Bloomington
Saint Paul School of Theology	John Skubal Johnson County Community College
Saint Vincent de Paul Regional Seminary	Mike Nickell Embry-Riddle Aeronautical University
Trinity Evangelical Divinity School	John Harrod Northern Illinois University, and Ron Ripley Marquette University
Trinity Lutheran Seminary	James Stevens The Ohio State University

Institution	Evaluator
Union Theological Seminary	William Farrell CUNY/Brooklyn College
University of Saint Mary of the Lake	Joseph Kish Northeastern Illinois University
Western Evangelical Seminary	Howard Wells Oregon State University
Weston School of Theology	Paul Barrett Massachusetts Institute of Technology
Yale University Divinity School	Douglas McKean Yale University

Glossary

Adaption expenditures   Expenditures required to adapt the physical plant as required to the evolving needs of the institution and to changing standards. These expenditures are over and above normal maintenance, are for items with a life cycle in excess of one year, and are not normally contained in the annual operating budget.

Alterations   Work that is required because of a change in use of the facility or a change in program.

Condition assessment   A structured analysis of the comprehensive data base established from a facility condition inspection. The assessment is used to identify specific data areas and items to support individual requirements.

Condition inspection program   A continuous, systematic approach of identifying, assessing, prioritizing, and maintaining the specific maintenance and repair requirements for all facility assets to provide valid documentation, reporting mechanisms, and budgetary information in a detailed data base of facility concerns.

Current replacement value   The amount required to reproduce a facility in like kind and materials at one time in accordance with current market prices for material and labor.

Deferred maintenance   Maintenance projects from prior years and the current year that were not included in the maintenance process because of perceived lower priority status than those funded within available funding. Deferred maintenance includes postponed renewal and replacement maintenance and unperformed, unscheduled major maintenance.

Facilities audit   See Condition assessment.

Facilities equilibrium   The maintenance of the functional and financial value of institutional facilities over the long term, as defined in policy by the governing board (e.g., to maintain a facilities condition index rating of .05 or better for all campus facilities).

Facilities portfolio   The broad array of housing, laboratories, offices, classrooms, and other diverse facilities necessary to fulfill an institution's missions and objectives.

Facility condition rating   A numerical indicator formulated by the facility condition index. The rating system creates a subjective range of values to determine condition categories of good, fair, and poor.

New construction   Includes internal and external planning for new construction and small construction if funded out of current funds.

Normal maintenance   Systematic, day-to-day process funded by the annual operating budget to control deterioration of the facilities; e.g., structure, systems, equipment, pavement, and groups.

Renewal and replacement maintenance   Systematic management process to plan and budget for known future cyclic repair and replacement requirements that extend the life and retain usable condition of campus facilities and systems and are not normally contained in the annual operating budget. This includes major activities that have a maintenance cycle in excess of one year, e.g., replace roofs, paint buildings, resurface roads, etc.

Unscheduled major maintenance   Work that requires immediate action to restore service or remove anticipated problems that will interrupt activities.

Visual inspection   An evaluation of the physical condition of building components to determine maintenance and repair requirements by visual inspection and interview methods. This type of inspection does not include specialized metering, destructive testing, or disassembly of building components.

Bibliography

American Council on Education. "Special Focus: Rebuilding the Nation's Campuses." *Educational Record*, Winter 1989.

APPA: The Association of Higher Education Facilities Officers. *Comparative Costs and Staffing Report for College and University Facilities*. Alexandria, Virginia: APPA, biennial.

————. *Computer Applications*. (Critical Issues in Facilities Management series, #1.) Alexandria, Virginia: APPA, 1987.

————. *Work Control*. (Critical Issues in Facilities Management series, #2.) Alexandria, Virginia: APPA, 1988.

————. *Capital Renewal and Deferred Maintenance*. (Critical Issues in Facilities Management series, #4.) Alexandria, Virginia: APPA, 1989.

————. *Regulatory Compliance for Facilities Managers*. Alexandria, Virginia: APPA, 1989.

————. *Case Studies in Environmental Health and Safety*. Alexandria, Virginia: APPA, 1990.

————. *Energy Management*. (Critical Issues in Facilities Management series, #6.) Alexandria, Virginia: APPA, 1990.

————. *Management Basics*. (Critical Issues in Facilities Management series, #5.) Alexandria, Virginia: APPA, 1990.

————. *Planning, Design, and Construction*. (Critical Issues in Facilities Management series, #7.) Alexandria, Virginia: APPA, 1990.

————. *Asbestos in the Workplace: Managing Small-Scale Abatement*. Alexandria, Virginia: APPA, 1991.

————. *Facilities Renewal at the Small College*. Alexandria, Virginia: APPA, 1991.

————. *Facilities Stewardship in the 1990s*. Alexandria, Virginia: APPA, 1991.

————. *Physical Plant Job Descriptions*. Alexandria, Virginia: APPA, 1991.

————. *Preservation of Library and Archival Materials*. Alexandria, Virginia: APPA, 1991.

Bennis, Warren. *Why Leaders Can't Lead: The Unconscious Conspiracy Continues*. San Francisco: Jossey-Bass, Inc., 1989.

———— and B. Nanus. *Leaders: The Strategies for Taking Charge*. New York: Harper & Row, 1985.

Boyer, Ernest L. *College: The Undergraduate Experience in America*. New York: Harper & Row, 1987.

Carnegie Foundation for the Advancement of Teaching. "How Do Students Choose a College?" *Change*, January/February 1986.

Chait, Richard P. and Barbara E. Taylor. "Charting the Territory of Nonprofit Boards." *Harvard Business Review*, January-February 1989.

Christenson, James E. "Maintenance Management for the 1990s." *Facilities Manager*, Spring 1991.

Conway, Daniel P. "Stewardship of Seminary Facilities: Planning for the Future." *Facilities Manager*, Spring 1991.

Cotler, Stephen R. *Removing the Barriers: Accessibility Guidelines and Specifications*. Alexandria, Virginia: APPA, 1991.

DePree, Max. *Leadership Is an Art*. New York: Doubleday, 1989.

Dillow, Rex O., ed. *Facilities Management: A Manual For Plant Administration*, second edition. Alexandria, Virginia: APPA, 1989.

Dozier, John et al. *Operational Planning and Budgeting for Colleges*. Washington: National Association of College and University Business Officers, 1988.

Drucker, Peter. *Managing in Turbulent Times*. New York: Harper & Row, 1980.

Dunn, John A. Jr. *Financial Planning Guidelines for Facility Renewal and Adaption*. Ann Arbor, Michigan: Society for College and University Planning, 1989.

Education Writers Association. *Wolves at the Schoolhouse Door: An Investigation of the Condition of Public School Buildings*. Washington: EWA, 1989.

Fackler, F. Louis. "Alternate Financing of Campus Projects." In *Proceedings of the 71st Annual Meeting of APPA*. Alexandria, Virginia: APPA, 1984.

Farley, Edward. *Theologia: The Fragmentation and Unity of Theological Education*. Fortress Press, 1983.

Fisher, J.L. *The Power of the Presidency*. New York: ACE/Macmillan, 1984.

————. *The Board and the President*. New York: ACE/Macmillan, 1991.

Ford, Frederick R. "Policy-making Issues." In *Facilities Stewardship in the 1990s*. Alexandria, Virginia: APPA, 1991.

Forrester, Robert T. *A Handbook on Debt Management for Colleges and Universities*. Washington: NACUBO, 1988.

Gardner, J.W. *On Leadership*. New York: Macmillan, 1990.

Gretchen, Stephanie. "Ideas and Innovations: The Best From the 1989 Awards for Excellence." *Facilities Manager*, Fall 1989.

Gullette, Jon M. "Vanderbilt University's Deferred Maintenance Study." In *Proceedings of the 74th Annual Meeting of APPA*. Alexandria, Virginia: APPA, 1987.

Hawkey, Earl W. and Joseph Kleinpeter. *Computerized Management of Physical Plant Services*. Washington: APPA, 1983.

Hensell, Eugene. Unpublished lecture notes on planning, prepared for the APPA/Lilly Workshop on Seminary Facilities, May 1991.

Hough, Joseph C. Jr. and John B. Cobb Jr. *Christian Identity and Theological Education*. Scholars Press, 1985.

Houle, Cyril O. *Governing Boards*. San Francisco: Jossey-Bass, Inc., 1989.

Howard, Steve. "The Director as Planner: A Profile of Rhodes College." *Facilities Manager*, Spring 1986.

Jenny, Hans H., with Geoffrey C. Hughes and Richard D. Devine. *Hang-Gliding or Looking for an Updraft: A Study of College and University Finance in the 1980s—The Capital Margin*. Wooster, Ohio: The College of Wooster, 1981.

Kaiser, Harvey H. *Mortgaging the Future: The Cost of Deferring Maintenance*. Washington: APPA, 1979.

————. *Crumbling Academe: Solving the Capital Renewal and Replacement Dilemma*. Washington: Association of Governing Boards of Universities and Colleges, 1984.

————. *Facilities Audit Workbook: A Self-Evaluation Process for Higher Education*. Alexandria, Virginia: APPA, 1987.

Kershner, Earl Gene. "Why Do University Buildings Cost So Much?" *Business Officer*, April 1987.

Kotler, Philip and Alan R. Andreasen. *Strategic Marketing for Nonprofit Organizations*, third edition. New York: Prentice-Hall, 1987.

McClintock, David L. *Formula Budgeting: An Approach to Facilities Funding*. Washington: APPA, 1980.

McCullough, Jim and Pat Dennis. *Academic Research Facilities: Financing Strategies. Report of a Conference*. Washington: National Academy of Sciences, 1986.

Moore, April. "The Best in Service: Innovations From Award Winning Facilities." *Facilities Manager*, Fall 1990.

Moss, Marvin A. *Designing for Minimal Maintenance Expense: The Practical Application of Reliability and Maintainability*. New York: Marcel Dekker, Inc., 1985.

National Science Foundation. *Scientific and Engineering Research Facilities at Universities and Colleges: 1988*. Washington: NSF, 1988.

————. *Scientific and Engineering Research Facilities at Universities and Colleges: 1990*. Washington: NSF, 1990.

O'Neil, Robert M. "Facilities Role for Excellence in Higher Education." *Facilities Manager*, Fall 1989.

Patton, Michael Quinn. *Qualitative Evaluation and Research Methods*. Newbury Park, California: Sage Publications, 1980.

————. *Practical Evaluation*. Newbury Park, California: Sage Publications, 1982.

Peters, Tom. *Thriving on Chaos: Handbook for a Management Revolution*. New York: Alfred A. Knopf, 1988.

———— **and Robert H. Waterman Jr.** *In Search of Excellence*. New York: Harper & Row, 1982.

Rosenfeld, Beth A. "The Pursuit of Excellence in Facilities Management." *Facilities Manager*, Fall 1988.

Rush, Sean C. and Sandra L. Johnson. *The Decaying American Campus: A Ticking Time Bomb*. Alexandria, Virginia: APPA, 1989.

Rush, Sean C. et al. *Managing the Facilities Portfolio: A Practical Approach to Institutional Facility Renewal and Deferred Maintenance.* Washington: National Association of College and University Business Officers, 1991.

Saunders, Laura E. "The Politics of Budgeting for Deferred Maintenance." *New Directions for Institutional Research*, Spring 1989.

Schaw, Walter A. "The Time Bomb Continues to Tick." *Educational Record*, Winter 1989.

———. "Building for a Thousand Years." *Educational Record*, Summer 1990.

Schuth, Katarina. *Reason for Hope.* Glazier, 1989.

Senge, Peter M. "The Leader's New Work: Building Learning Organizations." *Sloan Management Review*, Fall 1990.

Sherman, Douglas R. and William A. Dergis. "Funding Model for Building Renewal." *Business Officer*, February 1981.

Vallet, Ronald E. *Stepping Stones of the Steward.* Grand Rapids, Michigan: William B. Eerdmans Publishing Company, 1989.

van der Have, Pieter. "Deferred Maintenance: A Rose By Any Other Name." *Facilities Manager*, Spring 1988.

Werner, Thomas. "Things Fall Apart." *American School and University*, February 1984.

Westerhoff, John H. III. *Building God's People in a Materialistic Society.* New York: Seabury Press, 1983.

Wilson, Linda S. "Planning for Excellence: The Capital Facilities Dilemma in the American Graduate School." *Planning for Higher Education*, Vol. 15, No. 1, 1987.